W9-CBP-864
College

THE
WALTER
LYNWOOD
FLEMING
LECTURES IN SOUTHERN HISTORY

Louisiana State University

OTHER PUBLISHED LECTURES IN THIS SERIES

RELIGIOUS STRIFE
ON THE
SOUTHERN
FRONTIER

RELIGIOUS STRIFE
ON THE
SOUTHERN
FRONTIER

WALTER
BROWNLOW
POSEY

louisiana state university press   *1965*

Copyright 1965 by
Louisiana State University Press

Library of Congress Catalogue Card Number: 65-16509

Manufactured in the United States of America by
Vail-Ballou Press, Inc., Binghamton, New York

Designed by Robert L. Nance

277.6
P85

Baker + Taylor

3.20

Mar. 31. 67

26728

To the memory of
WALTER LYNWOOD FLEMING
Teacher, Counselor, and Friend

ACKNOWLEDGMENTS

When I was asked to deliver the Twenty-fifth Series of the Walter Lynwood Fleming Lectures in Southern History at Louisiana State University in April, 1963, I gladly accepted the invitation. It was my good fortune to study under the guidance of Dr. Fleming; and in a very real sense these lectures belong to him, for it was he who urged me to make frontier religion the field of my research.

I should like to express my gratitude to the members of the faculty, the students, and the community of Louisiana State University for the many courtesies extended to Mrs. Posey and me during our very pleasant days on the campus. These lectures appear in print because a generous committee of the Louisiana State University Press deemed them worthy to be the eighteenth volume in this distinguished series of published lectures.

WALTER BROWNLOW POSEY

Agnes Scott College
and
Emory University

CONTENTS

INTRODUCTION

The history of the several Protestant churches which flourished on the Appalachian frontier provides no basis for the ecumenical movement that distinguishes the present era of the Christian religion. The denominations which dominated the scene in American life of the eighteenth and nineteenth centuries sharpened their dissimilarities, assumed attitudes of extreme antagonism toward each other, and shunned cooperation among themselves in order to reach a scattered folk. They found strength in exclusiveness, individualism, and eventually in divisiveness. Only during occasional periods of extraordinary stress did the several churches forget their singular positions and willingly blend their activities for a common benefit. These lapses from individualism occurred during the American Revolution, the era of the camp meeting, the epidemics of plague and fever in affected areas, and the period of the Civil War. After each merger of energy and emotion the churches, having been swept together by the undertow of the immediacy, then sought the solid ground of distinctiveness on which to stand again separate and apart.

In view of the lack of cooperation among the churches, interdenominational relations in the new regions of the West were frequently unpleasant and often displayed an unchristian sentiment. The relations easily became skirmishes—Protestants against Protestants, denominations against sects, and Protestants against Catholics. Such relations were wholly lacking in ecumenicity. "Into All the World Together" was not the motto on Protestant escutcheons.

In the course of these lectures some aspects of interdenominational relations among the several churches in the Old South will be examined. The scope of the study will extend from the early movement of folk into Kentucky and Tennessee to the later population spread into territories and states in the lower Mississippi Valley. The Presbyterian, Baptist, and Methodist churches usually got an early foothold in a new region; and, as they eyed each other suspiciously, they resolutely assumed the roles of competitors. As new sects came into an area, the churches resented each intrusion and attacked the intruder as a common enemy. When finally, through determination and endurance, the come-lately gained a place for itself, such as that which the Disciples of Christ achieved, time as an abrasive rubbed off the sharp edges and the Protestant churches added another member to their ranks. Since the Roman Catholic Church had early spent itself in the Gulf region, the Protestant churches counted the Catholic Church in that area as no threat to their supremacy. Wherever there were pockets of Catholicism, however, the Protestant churches presented themselves in a semblance of a united front.

The America which had loomed on the horizon as a haven for refugees from political imprisonment and religious restriction actually offered limited liberties to many people who settled in the thirteen English colonies. Only Pennsylvania had no laws discriminating against Catholics. Neither the English Toleration Act of 1689 nor the colonial statutes in conformity with that law extended relief to Catholics. The British had brought with them to America a deep-seated bias against the Catholics, and they often exercised it without moderation whenever events permitted. Such was the conduct of the Protestants in Maryland in the early eighteenth century, when, having gained control of the colonial government, they disfranchised the Catholics and forbade them the right of public worship. Prejudices prevailed in the English colonies even though Catholics composed a small minority of the total population. Although every one of the colonies had some type of religious discrimination, greater liberty actually existed than the laws and their enforcement seemed to indicate.

It had been the reasoning of some colonists that religion and morality could be best maintained by means of institutionalized churches supported by the colonial governments. Nine of the English colonies in America had Established churches—the Congregational in Connecticut, Massachusetts, and New Hampshire; the Church of England in New York (City and a few counties), Maryland, Virginia, North Carolina, South Carolina, and Georgia. In the four remaining colonies, the several dissenting religious groups strenuously demanded religious toleration and freedom.

Geography and climate were considerable factors in making for diversity. The geographical spread of the colonies at once introduced a variety in social life and fostered a change in intellectual processes. The compactness of the New England scene with village life and the scattered isolation of the Southern rural areas offered to the colonists no basis for homogeneity in thought and custom. The lack of transportation and communication contributed heavily to the growth of intolerance. Here was a paradox—the individual, wanting freedom from established orders and rules, became excessively suspicious of people unlike himself and intolerant of divergent philosophies and opinions.

In colonial Virginia a delightful story was circulated about an old woman, reared in the tradition and custom of the Anglican Church, who on seeing her first Baptists vowed "hardly any of them looked like other people." The hearer is not expected to accept the veracity of the descriptive phrases she used—"hair-lipped," "clump-footed," "blear-eyed," "bow-legged," and "hump-backed"—but he certainly gets the compounded idea that members of the Baptist congregations were unlike those of the Episcopal commune. Antagonism toward Baptists was severe in Virginia, but persecution was not new to members of the Baptist churches; such had been the treatment meted to them wherever they had settled. The opposition in Virginia was not identified with any one denomination or class, but members of the Anglican Church caused no small part of it. Worshipping assemblies were disturbed by ruffians, and preachers were imprisoned on warrants charging them with disturbance of the peace. James Madison wrote to a concerned friend about "the diabolical, hell-conceived principle of persecution" which was perpetrated by some members of the clergy in Virginia. He firmly believed that a multiplicity of sects would be the best means of securing and preserving religious liberties for Americans.

Each of the major dissenting groups in America was a copy of some church organization in England but held no closer relation to the European groups than a fraternal feeling. Actually, all the Protestant churches in America by spirit and practice were closer to each other than to their counterparts in Europe. Since the Anglicans were definitely a minority in the colonies, the Church of England in the Colonies was not an agency which promoted strong loyalty for the mother country. On the contrary, many of the congregations and their ministers, especially in New England, took the lead in proclaiming colonial rights and resisting any encroachment by the British. It is an arresting fact that two-thirds of the signers of the Declaration of Independence were nominally Episcopalians, and that more Episcopalians signed the Constitution of the United States than members of any other religious group. It may be surmised that such men were nonconformists in political theory only, holding strictly to the religious conservatism of the Book of Common Prayer.

Once the American Revolution had begun, hope for victory for the colonies rested on unity of effort which included a cessation of squabbling and the granting of tolerance by the religious groups. Immersed in fighting for some six years, church members faced the total involvement of being Americans rather than being Baptists, Methodists, Congregationalists, Presbyterians, Episcopalians, Quakers, or Catholics. The nation and the churches, driven by necessity and the truth of God's Word as interpreted chiefly by Baptists and Quakers, had decided for religious liberty. Indeed if the nation was now to be made holy, it could be done only by persuasion. No law reenforced the position of any church. Religious liberty was an elixir blended of problems and benefits; the churches faced their greatest opportunities and their greatest threats.

RELIGIOUS STRIFE
ON THE
SOUTHERN
FRONTIER

I

PROTESTANTS AGAINST PROTESTANTS

INDEPENDENCE OF THE AMERICAN COLONIES FROM
England freed the ineffectively organized churches
of many hampering restrictions. By the end of the colonial
period three principles had been generally accepted by
almost all religious bodies: religious toleration, equality of
all before the law, and separation of church and state. All
the colonies passed laws providing for freedom of worship
for Protestants; most of the old laws penalizing Catholics
were removed; complete separation of church and state
became a fixed privilege by 1833 when Massachusetts abol-
ished legal disabilities. The adoption in 1791 of the first
ten amendments to the Constitution of the United States
pointed the way to full religious liberty for all faiths. With

3

not more than one-third of the colonial population actively supporting the American Revolution, the record of the Catholics was as good as that of any other religious group, and, of course, far better than that of the Anglicans. Considerable headway in religious freedom for the American Catholics from European domination was evident in the consecration in 1790 of John Carroll as Bishop of Baltimore. His consecration had been delayed a year after his appointment, partly because Carroll desired to have omitted from his oath a medieval pledge to drive heretics out of his jurisdiction. This fair-minded and farsighted church officer continually sought for fifty years to preserve in the hearts of the Catholics under his care "a warm charity and forbearance toward every other denomination of Christians."

What was the condition of the Protestant churches after their struggle for religious liberty? Despite heavy losses the Presbyterian Church emerged from the American Revolution in good condition. Its members had been thoroughly American in their sympathies chiefly because they were descendants of Ulster Scots who had suffered from the English Episcopacy, religious persecution, and economic oppression first in Scotland and later in Ireland. The Baptists had been deadly earnest in their demands for religious liberty. Those unwavering individualists had suffered more than any other small Protestant denomination from Anglican intolerance. As late as 1774 Anabaptist preachers in Virginia had been imprisoned for failure to secure licenses to preach, and in Massachusetts Baptists had been jailed for evading church taxes. Although they had, like other denominations, lost buildings, they had enjoyed an increase in membership throughout the colonies.

Prejudices and suspicions hovered over the Methodist societies. All of the recently arrived Methodist preachers returned to England except Francis Asbury, who refused to take the oath of allegiance in Maryland and fled to Delaware where no oath was required. But the spirit of Methodism was not abandoned. Local leaders working against great odds claimed to have gathered ten thousand members into the scattered societies between 1775 and 1783. When the treaty was signed between the American colonies and England in 1783, the Church of England in the Colonies actually ceased to exist. Sentiments of loyalty to the British had destroyed its prestige and rendered its clergy objects of suspicion. Upon them fell the fury of patriot hatred. Many of the clergy fled to England, others to Canada, and others dropped from the church rolls. Some of the churches were closed, others were wrecked, and the land and the property were confiscated. The disestablishment had been completed. In 1789 the church took new form as the Protestant Episcopal Church, based on American rather than English standards.

The years immediately after the Revolutionary War saw heavy migration to the West, and as reports of cheap fertile land came back the movement of folk increased. The churches already with a good working organization set themselves to extend their programs and to send preachers to the people in the fertile valleys of the Ohio and Mississippi rivers. Failing to appraise the opportunities realistically, enthusiastic church leaders overestimated the appeal of religion for the land-hungry emigrants, many of whom had been landless or impoverished by war. Preachers found their welcome less warm than that extended to land agents or to speculators who told inviting tales of promised lands, more real than those in the sky. As man's opportunities for acquiring land increased, he turned his attention to the acquisition of other possessions; and for the while he permitted his normal regard for religion to fall under this unusual spirit of avarice and cupidity. He may have desired and implored some divine aid, but he directed his plea largely in behalf of his victory over forest and grassland. When he had more time, he would attend to the salvation of his soul. A preacher of one denomination was there today and gone tomorrow, and a representative of another church followed him. If the settler missed a religious experience of one sort, he could catch another next month, in the fall, or in the spring. He may not have pondered on the assortment of doctrines offered to him, but there were some thinking men who saw the state of religion being weakened by sectarianism, who saw "both the spirit and the practice of religion" being destroyed and lowered into contempt. Religious conditions in New England and along the Eastern seaboard were similar to those on the frontier. The widespread indifference to religion prompted Leonard W. Bacon, one of the early authorities on religion in America, to characterize the two decades after the American Revolution as "the lowest ebb-tide of vitality in the history of American Christianity."

A revolt against the prevailing religious orthodoxy led to the limited acceptance of Unitarianism, Universalism, and Deism. The French Revolution became a popular topic for conversation, and the religious skepticism associated with the movement attracted in the West numerous advocates of French "infidelity."

Some leaders in various churches in the East were unduly apprehensive that the West was fast becoming the great godless portion of America; and others, seeing the leveling forces of democracy at work, feared correctly that the balance of power would ultimately rest in the vast region beyond the mountains. As early as 1798 the General Assembly of the Presbyterian Church, concerned with the religious desolation of the West and a few pockets of infidelity and atheism, appointed a committee to inquire into the situation and to make provisions for missions. A few missionaries were sent, but the number was too small to touch the expanding human stream that had far exceeded the strength of the churches to supply the means of grace. When these missionaries arrived in their assigned regions, they found that some preachers and priests who went out with the first wave of settlers had preceded them. But these hardy preachers who had moved with the people were too few in number and were not always the most able to serve the people in the widely scattered settlements or to reach the daring folk who pushed beyond the fringe of communities.

Even where there was some concentration of population, the task of the preacher was not easy. Villages frequently were the meeting places of men fleeing from justice; some towns gained lasting notoriety because of the caliber of their less respectable citizens, who had little regard for religion, education, or any cultural enrichments. In some communities it was hard for a man of superior background and training to hold himself aloof from the ways of the majority. The preacher had to be both a part of and apart from the people he served. When settlers were spread over great space, distance was a barrier to the effectiveness of the preacher. He could not carry the gospel to a people with whom he had no contact, so it became his business to go to the people wherever he could find them—he traveled seeking people, and, finding them, he preached salvation and damnation with great emphasis on repentance of sins. He was well received by the few who heard him, but they were too few. The preacher needed to get the people together in large groups, for religious experiences were contagious and he needed help in infecting the hard of heart. Born out of necessities, camp meetings were a new way to preach the gospel and to provide the means with which to meet the indifference of the frontier. The camp site for a while usurped the place of the church building in Western society. Thoughtful observers have noted that religion does not continue at some intense heat, but after a period it tends to cool and later something happens to increase the temperature. The Western revival movement furnishes a perfect example of this point.

Introduced into Logan County, Kentucky, in 1797 by James McGready, a Presbyterian minister, the camp meeting caught hold instantly and swept a large area for several years. Literally thousands, some say twenty-five thousand, attended the great Cane Ridge meeting in Kentucky in August, 1801. At this enormous gathering six or seven preachers exhorted simultaneously at different places in the camp grounds and wrung from the crowds cries for forgiveness and mercy. As the camp meetings spread through the Western country, the great gatherings, uninhibited and highly emotional, surrendered themselves to religious excitement with little interest in theology. For the duration of the revival period Methodist and Baptist preachers joined the Presbyterians in a concerted effort to convince people of their sins and to turn them from their waywardness. This cooperation among the several denominations lasted as long as they were sure of each other's religious soundness. Attacking the devil and infidelity, the revivalists presented an emotional appeal and expected in return a gripping emotional experience. This the frontiersman liked: damnation and salvation were spelled out to him in graphic terms, and his choice was uncluttered with intellectualism. Very likely he had lived a strenuous and even violent life, and by temperament he reacted affirmatively to an emotionally strenuous religious life.

These revivals enabled the several churches in the West to reach the masses of people and to win them for their own. A converted person did not automatically become a member of a church; he was won by persuasion to a specific denomination, or the church gained no members. And the art of persuasion was no gentle one. Distinctive features, obviously insignificant as they might be with respect to eternal truths, were stressed as means of saving grace. Every denomination became involved beyond reason in conversion—the means to the end for which all strived. At first the older Presbyterian ministers took the lead in the camp meetings, but as the theological emphasis of the revivals turned in the direction of Arminianism, most of the ministers with Calvinistic backgrounds gave way to younger ministers with a minimum of predestinarian theology. The very nature of revivals required of many ministers a lowering of pulpit standards in order to accomplish the needed immediate conversion with tears, remorse, and guilt. Furthermore, a semblance of cooperation among all denominations was absolutely necessary. Such a mutual endeavor meant relinquishing accustomed ways, the loss of which threatened the very distinctiveness of a church such as that of the Presbyterian.

Soon Methodist preachers were in control of the camp meetings, either by virtue of their aggressiveness or by right of possession; and their predominance hastened the withdrawal of the Baptist preachers who had far less in common with the Methodists than with the Presbyterians. Although the most insignificant of all sects at the close of the Revolution, the Methodist Church had shrewdly adapted itself to the frontier and had seized control of the most effective method of evangelization ever contrived. As the conserative elements of the Presbyterian and Baptist denominations withdrew their support of camp meetings, liberal groups ready to break with their historical theology cooperated with the Methodists, diluted their Calvinism with free will, and won for themselves such descriptive names as Cumberland Presbyterians, Stoneites, and New Lights. Evidence is abundant and convincing that the early revivals had little appreciable effect on the upper brackets of social life. The Episcopalians and the Catholics withheld their participation in the movement and indicated little interest.

The revival movement, largely in the form of camp meetings or protracted meetings, carried most of the West in its wake and recurred at intervals on new frontiers. Its aim remained constant: to admit the individual to church membership and to assure his conformity to accepted standards of conduct. His religious life at once became public property, and the church of his choice reserved the right to question and to guard his behavior. Meditation and spirituality had no more part in his subsequent religious life than theology had had in his conversion.

Theological differences had been reduced to a minimum by the preachers and the leaders in the effort to encourage cooperation among the Protestant churches and to insure wholesale conversions at camp meetings. "The religious holiday" reached its peak about 1805 and 1806. When the time came to count the fish caught in the gospel net, the inevitable result was strife, schism, diversion, and new sects—some ultimately destined to become new denominations. So strong were the tendency and the inclination toward schism that between 1790 and 1830 all major denominations in the West experienced one or more divisions because the main body of each church had not been able or did not choose to keep abreast of the radical spirit of the region. The great size of the country encouraged diversity of churches, and groups continued to break away until the pressing demands were met by change and innovations.

Among the three major churches only the Methodist escaped a damaging schism. By 1792 James O'Kelly, protesting against the power of the bishop, had fomented a rift and gathered some adherents; but these Republican Methodists did not actually disrupt the parent organization. The solidity of the Methodist Church may be attributed to its recent organization with features that suited a new land and to the administrative efficiency of Bishop Francis Asbury. As late as 1850 Episcopal Bishop Benjamin B. Smith, in an address to the Diocese of Kentucky, warned against the disastrous results of continuing divisions among sects and denominations. He was sure that most of the Western sects were no longer occupied in the defense and propagation of their own distinctive views but had busied themselves with "paltry distinctions, to the sad neglect of the weightier matters of our common Christianity." Many years would pass before American churches would learn the advantage of cooperation in a broad effort to spread Christianity. By the time the national churches had adapted themselves to the expanding frontier, they were suffering divisions over the slavery issues.

The Presbyterian and Congregational churches had little interest in competing for the unchurched on the frontier. They were concerned over the "desolated wastes" to which their members and those of like mind were moving and felt a responsibility to go with them to these new lands. For many years the Calvinistic Congregationalists in New England and the Presbyterians in New York and the middle Atlantic states had found themselves moving toward a common basis of unity. In 1801 they entered into a Plan of Union, designed chiefly for sparsely settled regions, by which members of the two denominations could form a single congregation and could call an available minister from either denomination. Although they held different views on church government, the two groups were close on several points. A genuine bond existed in their insistence on sending only thoroughly educated ministers to function as preachers and teachers on the frontier.

Ideally, the plan was good and provided a stretching of the scant supply of trained ministers. However, in practice the union smothered denominationalism, and some conservative Presbyterians were not content with a hybrid congregation. The traditional ways of the church were being lost, said the Old School party of the Presbyterians; and this complaint was repeated and magnified until it became a matter of real discord between two factions in the Presbyterian Church. Although terminating in disunion, the Plan of Union was a significant effort in cooperation, having had its most effective reach in the Midwest but scarcely operating at all south of the Ohio River. Conceived as a joint program between two churches, it functioned for thirty-six years as a competitor for other denominations which sought a place in the West.

The territorial expansion of the United States in the first quarter of the nineteenth century opened such vast lands for settlement that individual churches among the pioneer folk were powerless to keep step with population shifts. Protestants in the older states were so appalled at the prospects of the middle valley of America being left to barbarism, infidelity, and Romanism that they entered into some cooperative missionary efforts to combat all three. Almost within a decade a variety of Bible, tract, and missionary societies came into being. All orginated in the East and received direction and financial support from congregations and leaders in that section. Designed to provide destitute areas with preachers, schools, Bibles, and religious literature, the societies were never received as heartily as they had been conceived. The beneficiaries of these noble gestures too frequently warded off generosity and regarded interest as curiosity and helpfulness as meddlesomeness. The impact of the several missionary societies was negligible on the lower half of the Mississippi Valley.

In 1810 the Congregational Church formed the American Board of Commissioners for Foreign Missions whose chief aim was the advancement of missionary work among the Indians. It became interdenominational in 1812 by the election of some Presbyterians to its board. Although success was difficult to assess because the number of Indians who joined any church was small, some favorable gain seems to have accompanied this enterprise. The American Home Missionary Society, likewise interdenominational, was founded in New York in 1826 by delegates from the Presbyterian, Congregational, Dutch Reformed, and Associate Reformed denominations. Open rupture between Old School and New School Presbyterians in 1837 caused the withdrawal of Presbyterians from the support of the American Home Missionary Society.

As a preliminary to organization of some sort of vehicle for supplying Bibles in the West, Daniel Smith and Samuel J. Mills toured the Southwest in 1814 and 1815. The conditions they found affirmed the rumors that had prompted their trips. In a town of three thousand in Kentucky Saturday and Sunday were alike, except that on Sunday people were more noisy, profane, and wicked. Mills reported that in Louisiana he found families who had never seen a Bible and that no copy for sale or distribution could be found in New Orleans. This alarming report led to the formation in New York in 1816 of the American Bible Society, pledged to circulate Bibles "without note or comment."

In 1824 the growing interest in the Sunday school movement resulted in the organization in Philadelphia of the American Sunday School Union, a nonsectarian body. By publishing two magazines it promoted religious instruction and pious reading. Later its program included a plan to establish a Sunday school in every Western settlement which had none. In 1833 the South was specified as an open field. A kindred organization for the dissemination of religious literature for adults and children was organized in New York in 1825 as the American Tract Society. Having no denominational connections, the society could publish nothing that was unacceptable to any of its supporters.

These and other national organizations of similar nature held annual meetings simultaneously in the same place in order to benefit from each other's work. This cooperation on occasions led to the transference of funds from one agency to another when there was pressing need. Although they had no official connection with any denomination, the societies received most of their support from the Presbyterian, Congregational, and Unitarian churches. With their clergies exhorting congregations to pour money, missionaries, and teachers into the West, it was but natural that some opportunists, traveling in the guise of agents, contaminated the cause with overemphasis on money. In 1835 there were no less than twenty-three agents in New England begging for the West. The same attitudes of cooperation and competition, apparent on the camp ground, were hatched in the warm nest of mutuality.

Contrary to original intention, the several societies had short duration in the salubrious climate of cooperation. Denominational lines began to harden almost as soon as the missionaries sent by the American Home Mission Society reached the West. The Congregational and Presbyterian ministers had little respect for the Methodist and Baptist preachers, and propinquity lessened it no whit. Despite the fruitful efforts of the Methodist and Baptist preachers who had, as a rule, preceded them, the missionaries sent back to their home offices reports of destitute conditions and gloomy outlooks. Presbyterians, Methodists, and Baptists again vied for frontier supremacy. The "home grown" preachers resented the intrusion of the educated Eastern missionaries, and the need for them seemed far less than the parent societies had appraised. Leadership, inadequate and poor in quality as it was, could be found among the Westerners; and outside interference brought the local man into a favorable light.

In stating his opinion of missionaries from the East, a Baptist preacher revealed his own faults and his own uneasy position as "a plain old man": "I don't know nothing about them missionaries that go off to the heathen yonder,

. . . but what must they come amongst us for? If we allow them to come into our churches, the people will all go to hear them preach, and won't go to hear us preach, and we shall all be put down." Prejudice was strong in the Southwest against any newfangled notions. It was there that Baptists, Cumberland Presbyterians, and Disciples of Christ, all with untrained exhorters, opposed seminaries and missions on the grounds that God did not need any of them to convince sinners to mend their ways or to call a preacher. Ignorance and prejudice closed the minds of people in other sections also. In 1830 the Apple Creek Baptist Association in Illinois declared "an unfellowship with foreign and domestic missionary and bible societies, Sunday schools and tract societies, and all other missionary institutions." And to make sure that no help was given to such organizations, it further advised against contributing to "any such beggarly institutions."

The reaction of the Methodist Church to the Sunday school movement is a typical attitude toward a broad national program. The local churches had registered no interest in any educational endeavors. For some reason a gathering of children on Sunday was considered a desecration of the day. In 1822 a Methodist church in Nashville displayed a placard saying, "No desecration of the holy Sabbath, by teaching on the Sabbath in this Church." Hoping to rouse some new interest, the General Conference of 1824 specified that it was the duty of all preachers to form classes for children, but the resolution prompted little action.

Threatened by activity of the American Sunday School
Union and unwilling to be absorbed in a cooperative program, the Methodists established their own Sunday School
Union in 1827 and incorporated it with the whole system
of ecclesiastical and pastoral work. That independent step,
however, did not silence the smoldering opposition to
union endeavors; and one citation will illustrate the un-
reasonable complaints. In 1829 a correspondent to the
Holston Messenger expressed his opinion that the liberties
of the country had been disturbed by religious combina-
tions in union societies.

It should be said for the Methodists that they had somewhat balanced their neglect of formal education by providing an early supply of reading material. A "Book Concern"
had been established in 1789 in Philadelphia, and a branch
was located in Cincinnati in 1820 so that the Western readers could be better served. The American Bible and tract
societies supplemented in a great measure the literature
distributed by the Methodist book rooms. It was the duty
of every Methodist preacher to carry pamphlets or books
to sell on his circuit. Having acted as an agent for years,
James B. Finley, in autobiographical reflections, was not
sure of the wisdom of his role: ". . . I have wondered if the
great multiplication of books has not had a deleterious
tendency, in diverting the mind from the Bible; just as the
multiplicity of benevolent associations has a tendency to
divert the mind from the Church."

Despite an overlapping in the expenditure of money

and effort, the Baptists were not willing to throw in their lot with that of the American Tract Society. In 1824 the American Baptist Publication Society was organized with the stated purpose of being "a center round which the Baptists of every section might rally, a fountain from which should go out streams of blessings to every corner of the land." A gratuitous distribution may have accounted for part of the great demand which came to the publishing house, but good business conditions alone could justify the location of book depositories at Nashville in 1839 and at Mobile in 1842.

Among the major churches in the Southwest only the Presbyterian Church maintained good relations with the societies designed to aid frontier needs. The Presbyterians, already possessing a denominational consciousness that other churches were struggling to obtain, could chance or risk absorption in a common endeavor. A case in point is their contribution to the American Bible Society: in men and means the Presbyterian Church gave more than any other American church.

No voice of prejudice was louder than that of the stout controversialist, "Parson" William G. Brownlow, coming from an isolated pocket in the hills of East Tennessee. As a Methodist preacher, politician, and newspaper editor he used superlatives with no modesty and laid hard words on his victim. Feeling nothing but derision for the Presbyterians, Brownlow applied irony and sarcasm in an attack on them, calling his book *Helps to the Study of Presbyterian-*

ism. In this tirade he denounced every agency in which the Presbyterians had a controlling or important stake. He charged that on the board of directors of the American Tract Society there were five Calvinists for each Arminian and that, under the provisions of the constitution, Diests and Universalists were competent to take charge of the society. Striking at the American Home Missionary Society, Brownlow said that it had sent "little college-bred chaps and theological scavengers" through the West "prowling and skulking about our country, from one rich neighborhood to another, making proselytes and begging money." He accused the American Bible Society of being entirely under the control of the Presbyterians and the Congregationalists who claimed to have furnished the poor with Bibles. After examining an annual report of the society, Brownlow learned that the society had distributed gratis only 7,260 of the 134,629 copies printed. In terms of the society's income, he calculated that each free Bible had represented $8.91 in cash value. Then in order to clinch his point, he cited the cheap production costs of the Methodist Book Concern. He declared that missionaries sent by the American Board to East Tennessee had no interest except "mercenary motives to enrich themselves on the spoils of the simple natives."

Brownlow's savage attacks on institutions dominated by the Presbyterian-Congregational combination bear evidence that he may not have been as much opposed to the various societies as he was to the Presbyterians. It is doubtful that others feared them as much as did Brownlow, but there is ample evidence that many people believed denominations had lost identity in cooperating with others. The rapid organization of separate missionary, tract, Bible, and other societies; the establishment of schools, colleges, and publishing houses; and the founding of seminaries—all speak of the struggle for denominational identity, for identity regained or newfound.

When replying to a request for a union meeting, James B. Finley minced no words about cooperative projects with the Presbyterians: "I plainly told my brethren I had nothing against the Presbyterians; I loved them, but I loved Methodism more, and, as we had a shop of our own, we would not work journey-work any longer." Then directing his words to some Methodists who had been inclined toward union activity he shifted into the second person pronoun saying, "You can not pray aloud; and if one of you should get happy, you must quench the Spirit; or if you take a Methodist shout, they will carry you out as a disturber of the peace; besides, you dare not even to say amen above a whisper."

The Methodists were aggressive in their search for converts: they purposely sought to make Methodists out of whomever they might find and acted without any regard to priority which an established church might have in a section. Competing for "the less prosperous and the less cultured," the Methodists and the Baptists tore into each other's ranks with little respect for ethics or courtesy. The

Presbyterian churches often found themselves on the defensive, protesting that a community was theirs and protecting it from those preachers who rode in, made converts, and rode out leaving a disturbed and restless people. In 1812 Peter Cartwright, preaching on a Methodist circuit in Kentucky and Tennessee, offered strong competition to a stationed preacher whose Presbyterian congregation, although small, was housed in a brick edifice. Realizing that the Presbyterian ranks would be shattered if a Methodist church were organized, the minister pleaded with Cartwright to abandon his plan. Heedlessly Cartwright gathered a congregation with twenty-seven members, thirteen of whom had left the Presbyterian Church without letters of dismissal. Having lost his means of financial support, the Presbyterian minister moved on to Missouri.

As if needing elbowroom, the denominations shoved and pushed, attracted and repelled each other like children. This interplay of activities produced a set of relationships which attracted denominations to each other, then set them at cross purposes, and finally bred suspicion, jealousy, and and deep-seated antipathies. In time, as the Methodists and the Baptists lined themselves up as the chief contestants for converts, these two denominations developed strong dislikes for each other. Of course, the Baptists made much of the powerless local congregations of the Methodist Church and indulged in broad contrasts between their free and independent churches and those of the Methodists which were controlled by the bishop, the presiding elder, and the conference. Enjoying this game of taking the Methodists to pieces, some Baptists bragged about being "Arminian skinners" and in the skinning chose to spell out the despotism of the circuit rider who had the power to extend or to deny membership—such power, they insisted, was even more despotic than that of the Pope. The Baptists unwittingly grew in harmony with the Presbyterians because of their mutual Calvinism. The Presbyterians pulled back from the Baptists who uncompromisingly rejected infant baptism, open communion, and token baptism. The effective organization of the Methodist Church gave this denomination an advantage over the Baptist churches which were somewhat hampered by their loose form of government. The freedom of individual Baptist churches was a point in their favor, but it also left the gate wide open for dissensions and defections among themselves. When the Triennial Convention of the Baptist churches in 1817 made extensive plans for missionary work in the West, it hardly expected the opposition that came to it from congregations and preachers in the lower South. The program was sound and was being received in some degree when it collided with the antimissionary movement based on resentment of outside aid and assistance. This opposition arose largely from a fear of centralized authority and the notion that missions were money-getting schemes. Jealousy is not to be overlooked as a contributing factor; the illiterate and unpaid preacher had nothing but enmity for the trained and salaried missionary who was sent to the

West. The wag who said the churches fought the devil, other churches, and themselves spoke knowingly.

A point of attack between Methodist and Baptist congregations quite naturally lay in the diverse methods of baptism, a ritual magnified beyond its intrinsic value. The Baptists accepted plenary immersion as the only form of baptism sanctioned by the Scriptures and considered the sprinkling done by the Methodists as being too skimpy to wash away any sins. The frontier preacher transferred to the overt act of baptism all the redemptive powers he had claimed for the emotional experience of conversion. This confusion between the spirit and the symbol was apparent to many discerning men, but none saw it more clearly than Nicholas H. Cobbs, Episcopal Bishop of Alabama. Having a great dislike for the ceremony of immersion, Cobbs finally agreed to baptize two women in that fashion on two conditions—that the baptism should take place at dawn and that only the immediate family should be in attendance. Knowing full well that such conditions "took the glory" out of the baptizing, he was not surprised when the women cancelled their request. The Methodists, having adopted the Episcopalian manner of sprinkling with water as the necessary token of admission to church membership, heaped all manner of ridicule on the Baptists for their notions about the regenerating power of water.

The Presbyterians, who like the Methodists used water sparingly, tired of the Baptists' emphasis on baptism and accused them of being "incessant, extravagant, and clamor-

ous on the subject of immersion." Such talk led easily to
much disputation, and on the subject of baptism the
Presbyterians and the Baptists met often in debates without
proper Biblical exegesis. When Robert Grundy invaded
a Baptist territory in Kentucky to preach against immersion, it may be surmised that he performed well, for the
reply of the Baptists was given by William Vaughan, an
able and long-winded defender, who in a six-hour sermon
exhausted both his audience and his subject. Doubtless
one Presbyterian observer had just sat through a similar
lengthy discourse when he was prompted to observe that
"the Baptists suffer the water to extinguish the fire."

On the doctrine of infant baptism the Presbyterians
and the Methodists together met the assault of the Baptists.
The Regular Baptists, asserting there was no scriptural
basis for infant baptism, contended that the two denominations which administered it granted church membership
to unregenerated members. The Presbyterians regarded
the Baptist insistence on adult membership as "a constant
affront to those who considered the household the unit
of the covenant." Cartwright and an unnamed Baptist
preacher agreed to debate the subject of infant baptism
at a Methodist camp meeting. Debates were always crowd-
gathering devices, and the preachers who without restraint
or discretion championed their own cause and without
conscience attacked the beliefs of their spiritual rivals
could count on a good audience. These vigorous religious
debates lent zest to the uninteresting routine of daily life.

It is to be doubted, however, that the debates wrought any lasting effects or materially aided a hearer to reach a decision about his religious life.

Although the Presbyterians argued with the Baptists over their practice of close communion, the Presbyterians sought distinctiveness in the rules with which they "fenced the table" of Holy Communion. At regular intervals the session of the local church tested the entire church membership on the articles of faith and acquaintance with the Scriptures. Members who satisfied the examiners received tokens of metal or wood which gave them admittance to the communion table, and these tokens were collected prior to the distribution of the elements.

The celebration of the Lord's Supper provided many points of distinctions and of disagreements among the denominations. The minute details of communion became so involved with whom the church members should share the elements that in the process of decision charity went out the door. The Baptists who broke bread and sipped the wine with none but the Baptists, and not all of them, accomplished a degree of separation that barred any co-operative enterprise with other denominations. An effort for interdenominational union in Georgia failed because the Baptists feared such a project would lead to a relaxing of the regulations on the sacraments of baptism and holy communion. They forbade their members to attend the popular love feasts of the Methodists. One association in Kentucky made a formal statement saying that it was "a

transgression of the rule of the baptist [sic] in this union
for their meeting to participate with the Methodists in
what is called their love feasts." In retaliation to this
attitude some Methodist conferences ruled that those
Baptists who refused to "eat" with Methodists would not
be invited to fill their pulpits.

The Methodist Church, an autocratically governed
church with a democratic religion and a spiritual warmth,
did very well for itself in the West. Few Methodist preachers were capable of defining Arminianism, many stumbled
over the pronunciation, and a rare one could spell it; but
every circuit rider could expound for hours on man's
mastery of his own destiny. Arminianism, a theological
position which allowed the cooperation of an individual
in his own salvation, was more at home in the West than
was Calvinism, a doctrine whose supporters logically contended that revivals constituted a sheer waste of one's
time. In contrast to the stern unrelenting God of the
Presbyterians, the Methodists depicted Him as the
searcher of wayward men, of whom the woods were full.
The wide play which the followers of Wesley gave to
"salvation by faith" had great appeal; and while the Methodists counted their growing membership, it mattered not
if the Presbyterians called them "false prophets" and the
Baptists shouted, "Impostors." The Calvinist doctrine was
too cold and unpalatable for frontiersmen whose ears still
rang with talk of individualism and equalitarianism.
Lorenzo Dow, an eccentric evangelist of early Methodism,

aptly stated the frontier case against Calvinism in a four-
line jingle:

> You can and you can't
> You will and you won't
> You'll be damned if you do
> You'll be damned if you don't.

Couching his criticism in more elegant phrases than Dow's,
Timothy Flint, a Congregational minister serving many
Western communities, said that he preferred "to believe
in the utter annihilation of the soul, than in the gloomy &
horrible dogmas" of Calvinism which of all religions was
"the most abhorrent, the most dishonorable to the Divin-
ity & right reason."

Such was the doctrinal fare offered to the unchurched
Westerner. The future lay with the religious bodies that
could most effectively appeal to the rank and file, to the
man of mediocre equipment. Doctrinal shifts would be
made in order to gain an advantage in the denominational
struggle. In doctrinal quarrels the Presbyterians wasted a
vast amount of energy that might have been directed toward church expansion. In order to offset the freewill
gospel of the Methodists, the Baptist churches held high
the banner of Calvinism. The presence of this doctrine in
the body of Baptist beliefs has been the subject of much
discussion. It was a new element arising from a peculiar
frontier situation. Leonard W. Bacon offers no explanation

for the turning of the American Baptists to Calvinism "except the reaction of controversy with the Methodists." Despite their wide variances, the evangelical messages of the Methodist and Baptist churches fell on receptive ears and offered comfort and hope to the man who in moving westward had illusions of quick and easy success. Harsh reality brought preachers into new focus and kind lights.

The Baptists did not frequently mention the faults of their own preachers, but the Presbyterians were always aware of the poor qualities of the Baptist preachers and have left permanent records of these observations. A Presbyterian visiting in a section of Kentucky found thirty Baptist preachers there and not "a well educated man in the whole number." He observed that the popular attitude was "to cry down learning and salary for a gospel ministry, as an abomination not to be borne." Certain aspects of Calvinism made it easy for the person without formal training to refuse to support schools and theological seminaries, for such institutions implied the inadequacy of God to call and equip ministers. What more could any preacher need than a call to preach, inspiration from the Holy Spirit, and ability to quote scripture? Resenting any efforts to educate the Baptist clergy, one old preacher boasted that as long as he had wind he had no need for an education. This scorn of education was again witnessed by an agent of the Bible Society, a Presbyterian minister who was seeking subscriptions in Kentucky. He told of presenting his cause at the Mays Lick Baptist Church. Following the visitor's address, the local preacher, "with the appropriate dignity of an ignorant Baptist clergyman," made some inane remarks about the Bible, then laid two half-dollars on the table with the air of a job well done.

The educational superiority of the Presbyterian ministers gave them no immunity to criticism from the Baptists and the Methodists. From Cartwright came sharp remarks about manufactured ministers who read "old musty and worm-eaten sermons," and about eager young ones who might be improved "If they would tarry in Jericho till their beards were grown out. . . ." While on a missionary tour in Tennessee in 1828, Elijah Goodwin, a New Light preacher from Ohio, heard a Methodist preacher criticize the college-bred Easterners who had "a machine for making preachers." The Methodist Church, he insisted, wanted only "Holy-Ghost made preachers." The period of learning in a theological school was regarded with little respect by William G. Brownlow. He considered it as a needlessly long incubation, and with vividness he described the president of a Presbyterian seminary as "setting over a nest, warming and stirring his eggs, and hatching out *preachers.*" He noted that one of the seminarians, previously having been denied admittance to the Methodist ministry, was so long in hatching that he finally emerged with a "faint and feeble" intellect hidden in a "quantity of beef above his eye-brows." Delicacy was never a characteristic of the Parson.

In strict fairness mention should be made of the many

preachers who having been called to preach felt their inadequacy for the task and wanted earnestly to be prepared for it. None has stated the press of the moment better than Jacob Young, a willing servant of the Methodist Church in Kentucky. The year was 1801, a people were waiting for evangelization, and the supply of preachers was discouragingly low; the opportunity would pass if the church had to wait for a trained ministry. Such was the reasoning with which William McKendree, then a presiding elder, urged Young to forsake an education and to enter the ministry with only his natural gifts.

Some denominations were skeptical about the meager endowment of Methodist preachers as a whole and were curious to know the reason for their effectiveness. When inquirers willingly looked beneath the surface defects, they found a sincerity that was the key to the successful preaching of untrained men. An early North Carolina Presbyterian minister, a graduate of Princeton, observed the Methodists at work and made mention in his diary of their inherent power: "The strong sense of a present God and of accountability to him wh[ich] characterized the Methodists; the fervent spirit of devotion wh[ich] they carried into everything; and the earnestness with wh[ich] they preached the doctrine of justification by faith and of a free salvation, preaching it every where as if they hear the halleluiahs of heaven above and the groans of despair beneath, enabled an ignorant, blundering kind of speaker to melt and thrill and subdue a far more intelligent audience than himself." Thomas Cleland, a Presbyterian minister in Kentucky, found many scattered settlements in which there was no preaching except by Methodists who managed to find a preacher for every new settlement. In 1810 he wrote to a friend in Philadelphia that the Methodists "are very industrious in endeavoring to prepossess the minds of the ignorant and informed against every denomination but their own. They make preachers so much faster than we do, that they always get the start in those vacancies."

Ubiquity was an asset for any denomination. To be on the scene gave any preacher a head start in the community regardless of whatever doctrinal leaning the inhabitants might have. A quick wit and a sharp tongue were more effective tools of persuasion than a mind clogged with logic, doctrine, and dogma. The ever increasing membership of the Methodist and Baptist churches gave witness to the fact that their preachers spoke a simple understandable message and that they were committed to proselytism.

The Protestant Episcopal Church offered little competition to those denominations which strove among themselves. The impact of its few preachers and few churches was so slight that it was scarcely perceptible. Handicapped by its former connections with the Anglican Church, accused of lack of loyalty to the new democratic society, and suspected of Catholic rituals, the Episcopal Church half-heartedly faced the problems of the frontier and, realizing its limitations, let other denominations scramble for the converts.

But the Episcopal Church did not escape divisive factors within its structure. Its unity, while not tested to a breaking point, was sorely tried by the High Churchmen and the Low Churchmen, whose conflicting interpretations of the church as an institution caused a regrouping of its communicants. Because of their emphasis on "Gospel preaching," the Low Churchmen were known as the Evangelicals and felt a greater kinship with Protestants of other denominations than did the High Churchmen, who were "Fond of representing the Church as standing midway between Protestant error and Roman corruptions." More specifically, the High Churchmen were sectarian and conservative, and the Low Churchmen liked to unite with members of other denominations in their services and organizations.

The very nature of the Episcopal service repelled the uneducated, for those who cannot read are not inclined to prove their ignorance. The literary beauty of the Prayer Book offered no "springs of refreshment" to a man of meager education or to one unfamiliar with the service. In fact, the occasional drifter who through curiosity attended an Episcopal service found the brief, well organized sermon dull and, as he nodded in boredom, longed for the gesticulating delivery of the Methodist and Baptist preachers. One natural description which an ignorant man was heard to use of the service was, "Come, let us go and hear that man preach, and his wife jaw back at him." He referred to the responses made by Mrs. James H. Otey, who was often the only respondent in her husband's congregation.

Having a traditional fear of emotionalism, the Episcopalians were repulsed by the zeal of the Methodists but at the same time yearned for a modicum of it. So indicated Bishop Benjamin B. Smith, who, on seeing his church at a standstill, wished for a return of the Methodists to the Episcopal fold. This was but wistful thinking on the part of the individual. However, an earlier proposal for reunion of the splinter and parent groups had come in 1791 from Thomas Coke, Bishop of the Methodist Church. His suggestion fell on the receptive ears of Bishop William White and Bishop James Madison, both of whom knew the Methodists well and appreciated their zeal; but no actual steps were taken toward uniting the two denominations. After the Methodists began to scatter their poorly educated preachers over the countryside, Coke's suggestion would have received but slight attention from the Episcopal leaders who had no enthusiasm for the Methodist preachers, elevated from the laity with little or no schooling. Perhaps the Anglican Bishop Samuel Horsley stated best the general attitude of many Episcopalians toward the Methodist clergy: "The great crime and folly of the Methodists consist not so much in heterodoxy as fanaticism; not in perverse doctrine, but rather in a perverse zeal for the propagation of the truth, which is the pretense for that irregular ministry. . . ."

If the Episcopalians had chosen to enumerate the follies of the dissenters, certainly the revivals would have headed the list. The Episcopalians were actually frightened into helplessness by camp meetings. After witnessing the excitement at a meeting in Kentucky, an Episcopal minister marveled that "man can feed upon such unstable food. . . ." From Tennessee another observer called the revivals "the most fearful delusion," and others expressed their unwillingness to become involved in the meetings. This aloofness was regarded by the less sober denominations as a lack of sincerity. In fact, some people regarded Episcopalianism as being a spurious form of Christianity; and, if they needed proof of their point, the church's small membership was convincing evidence.

Long before the Episcopal Church reached Kentucky and Tennessee, people who had been confirmed and educated by it had wearied of waiting for the services of a clergyman and had united themselves with dissenting denominations. Although the overall governmental structure of the Episcopal and Methodist churches differed only slightly and both accepted the Arminian theology, the similarity of the two was seldom considered by the frontiersman. Actually the people in the Western settlements knew little about the historical structure of Methodism. Methodism to them was the circuit rider with the Bible and the Discipline; its theology was as slanted as the preacher's personal opinions. Mildly the preacher was for something, vehemently against something, and excessively loud in his denunciations. He soon learned that it was easier to attack his opponents than to defend his own position. Everyone knew what the Methodist preacher thought, and that was more than could be said of the Episcopal churchman whose devotion to the catholic aspects of his religion fashioned him seemingly without a notion of his own. When the slavery issue divided several churches, the ability of the Episcopalians to tolerate differences of opinion caused much speculation. This genius for toleration lessened the denominational distinctiveness on which many evangelical churches thrived. The term "Christian unity" had little meaning and less attraction for the man who had difficulty separating church and state.

When a revivalistic group, later identified as the Cumberland Schismatics, separated itself from the Presbyterians, only the Methodists gave encouragement to the new body. Despite the fact that a watered-down version of predestinarianism, having elements of both Arminianism and Calvinism, had been adopted by the Cumberland Presbyterians, the Methodists were unwilling to absorb the defectors and encouraged them to form a new church. Other factors besides the issue of doctrine contributed to the defection: these were insistence on the lowering of educational requirements for the ministry and controversy over the rights and powers of synods and presbyteries. For ten years controversy over the defectionists gave the old line Presbyterians opportunity to show the error of the waywards. Typical comments were the lacerations made by John Lyle, a hostile critic of the revival group. In 1805 Lyle spent two months in the bounds of the independent Cumberland Presbytery, which formed the nucleus of the Cumberland Presbyterian Church. He recorded his impressions of the new sect, saying that the preachers were "illiterate exhorters and licentiates," touched with Arminian sentiment, being no more than Methodist circuit riders. In order to show that the conduct of the new ministry was not in accordance with Presbyterian standards, Lyle described the actions of a Mr. Nelson who encouraged his congregation to shout, to pray aloud, or to do whatever they chose. From Tennessee another Presbyterian minister spared no words in describing the founders of the new sect as "three ignorant boys" who had "put to sea without chart or compass." And mixing his metaphors to the delight of his hearers, he likened the men to mushrooms which "would soon wither and die in the sunlight of Divine Truth."

Borrowing a great deal from the Methodists, the Cumberland Presbyterians made use of the anxious seat, the inquiry meeting, and the camp meeting. Converts came so rapidly to the new sect that conservative Presbyterians like James McGready expressed grave concern over the extreme position of the new group. "They have," he wrote to a friend, "a flame of animation . . . [which] supports them and gives them importance, but this malignant Spirit against the old Presbyterian . . . [seems] to differ from the Spirit of Christ. . . ." Many years passed before the Presbyterians were willing to "hold fellowship" with the Cumberlands, but this snubbing failed to kill the spirit of the new church which had sixty congregations within three years of its organization. This phenomenal growth continued, and by 1835 the church had three hundred ordained ministers and 75,000 communicants. Such success was the result of the blending of tried techniques under the able leadership and administration of Finis Ewing. The church adopted the revivalistic program and the circuit rider system of the Methodists and modified the Calvinistic creed to meet the needs of a frontier church. It had not been the original plan of the leaders to create a new church, but the intolerance of the Presbyterians did not allow enough cooling of tempers to prevent a complete separation.

The presence of two Shaker communities in Kentucky was almost ignored by the major denominations which contended for religious supremacy in the area. Outsiders called them Shakers because of their trembling during religious services, but the converts called themselves the United Society of Believers in Christ's Second Coming and saw their role as a lever to lift the rest of society nearer to God. It is surprising that the Baptists did not recognize some kinship to the Shakers whose practice of close communion in a marked degree had removed them from the world. Evidently the Baptists, seeing the small number of Shakers, brushed them aside as harmless competitors, too "wild and vague in their religious notions." Arriving in Kentucky in 1805, three Shaker missionaries found conditions so auspicious that nineteen more workers were sent from the East to organize societies or colonies. Between 1806 and 1810 the two Shaker communities of Pleasant Hill and South Union were erected and soon were filled to their capacity of six hundred and four hundred respectively. In such settlements the Shakers pursued their search for a perfect Christ-like society. Turning their backs on sex, marriage, private property, politics, and other concerns of the world, the Shakers made hard work a virtue and simplicity the test for all good things. Men of property and learning renounced the world and committed their all to the community. A great deal of Shaker success in the West turned around the conversion of two Presbyterians, Malcolm Worley, a prominent layman in Ohio, and Richard McNemar, an influential minister in Kentucky. According to Shaker testimony, Barton W. Stone, a Presbyterian revivalist whose inquiring mind would lead him down several intellectual roads, "sucked in our light as greedily as ever an ox drank water." Obviously Stone did not find the Shakers' philosophy of the divine order all that he sought, for he made no connection with them and chose to make other excursions from the Presbyterian fold until at last he came to rest among the Disciples of Christ.

The Disciples of Christ, a brotherhood of locally organized churches, represented the most typical form of Protestantism on the Southern frontier. Taking form under the leadership of Stone and Alexander Campbell, the sect emerged in the second quarter of the nineteenth century as a blend of Presbyterian, Baptist, and Methodist elements. Desiring to unite all Christians without the use of human creeds or denominational names, the founders claimed that they took their stance on the Bible and the Bible alone. Despite their dissociation with other Protestants, the Disciples of Christ owe much to the Presbyterian heritage of Stone and Campbell; to the Baptists with whom they shared an initial opposition to an educated ministry, Sunday schools, and missionary societies; and to the Wesleyan ideas which contributed to their doctrinal laxity. The Disciple brotherhood was a product of the conflicting influences which molded American Protestantism; it was the sum of the additions, the quotient of the divisions.

Having felt the physical drain which the Disciples made from the Baptist membership, the *Baptist Banner* (May 20, 1841) printed some strong comments on "Primitive Campbellism," as the editor phrased his title. A portion of his comments will indicate the spirit with which the come-lately denomination was greeted by its rivals: "We have often heard it suggested, that the spirit of fanaticism and excessive vanity by which the early advocates of this *no system* were distinguished, was a species of mania peculiar to the sect. For it mattered not how modest and retiring an individual was previous to his water-regeneration, he became immediately afterwards self-confident and noisy, and though as brainless as an empty gourd, panted for debate even with the most talented opponent, and though he could neither receive an idea nor impart one, always felt himself the victor for having made the loudest noise."

Harsh words and cold shoulders characterized the reception which the several Protestant denominations exhibited toward the newest addition to the religious forces of the West and the South. Despite boasts of tolerance and love of freedom, the American people rarely welcomed with enthusiasm a new religious group to the local scene. No good could come from innovators; and, if such a group gained maturity, the life process was the result of the survival of the fittest. Innovators, however, did not wait for warm receptions; free thinkers were at work in many places.

II

PROTESTANTS AGAINST A NEW SECT

THE WEST, THAT VAGUE AND INDEFINITE REGION THAT lay beyond the bounds of the early colonies and settlements, proved a fertile spawning ground for new sects, some of which under favorable conditions would grow into denominations. Ties of the newly organized Western churches to the East tended to weaken as they lengthened, for, once organized, the churches suddenly realized they could take care of themselves. The successful existence of some denominations depended on a flexible adaptation of creed and practice to a shifting people who, in some measure, sought escape from the old patterns of society. If a preacher, having adapted himself and his congregation too easily, should be censured by an Eastern synod or conference, he could repudiate authority and feel reasonably sure of some followers. If sufficiently encouraged and supported, the nonconformist might intentionally or unintentionally find himself the founder of a new religious organization. Once constituted the new sect, having sprung from the seedbed of toleration, must struggle for its continued existence among the tares of intolerance, prejudice, and resentment toward its very being. Wide as the Western lands were, they suddenly seemed too narrow for additional sects or denominations which at various times came into existence. The denominations, already well organized in the trans-Allegheny region of the United States, jealously resisted the encroachments of other church groups. In such an atmosphere in Kentucky, Tennessee, and other Western states arose numerous sects, the most important of which was a group called the Christians or the Disciples of Christ.

The towering and dominating figure in the reformation movement eventually to be known as the Disciples of Christ was Alexander Campbell. As a boy he was no stranger to religious controversy and political argument. His father, Thomas Campbell, came from a Scottish family long in residence in Ireland; and his mother had descended from a French Huguenot ancestry. After graduating from the University of Glasgow, Thomas Campbell became a minister in the Seceder Presbyterian Church, which had broken away from the Church of Scotland over certain relations between church and state. He became an avowed enemy of sectarianism and a firm advocate of Christian union. Leaving his family in Scotland, Campbell came to the United States in 1807 in order to find a better climate for his own health and better economic conditions in which to raise seven children. While waiting to join his father, Alexander studied at the University of Glasgow for a year and then, just barely twenty-one years of age, he brought the family to his father in western Pennsylvania in 1809.

Opposed to the religious intolerance in the region, Thomas Campbell declared himself free from the Presbytery of Chartiers and organized in August, 1809, the Christian Association of Washington (Pennsylvania). He proceeded at once to prepare the now famous *Declaration and Address,* a statement of principle and program for the association. Adopted and published before the end of 1809, this pamphlet of fifty-six pages has become the most important document in the history of the Disciples of Christ. It was the purpose of Campbell, with the aid of Alexander, to promote "a pure evangelical reformation" rather than to found a new religious group. Father and son both desired unity based on the Scriptures alone rather than on creed. Regardless of the aim, within two years the association constituted itself into the Brush Run Church and ordained Alexander Campbell in the ministry. Contrary to their original desire and purpose to promote reforms within the churches, the Campbells had constituted a congregation without the sanction of any ecclesiastical body or person except the thirty members of the recently organized Brush Run Church.

After the new church in 1813 had accepted plenary immersion as the proper scriptural mode of baptism necessary for the remission of sins, it applied for and secured membership in the Redstone Baptist Association. In this affiliation the new member protected itself with the reservation that always "we should be allowed to teach and preach whatever we learned from the Holy Scriptures, regardless of any human creed." In 1823 the Campbells and about thirty other members requested dismissal from the Brush Run Church in order to establish at Wellsburg, Virginia, a new congregation which promptly joined the Mahoning Baptist Association. Alexander Campbell, a man of ability, power, and ambition, assumed the leadership of this congregation—an arrangement which seemed agreeable with the elder Campbell. This tenuous union with the Baptists was maintained until about 1830 despite the leanings of Alexander Campbell toward Arminianism and his yet undefined notions on plenary immersion.

The spiritual climate of Kentucky likewise gave rise to to a movement somewhat similar to that of the Campbells. Seven years before the Brush Run Church had been organized, five former Presbyterian ministers in Kentucky, calling themselves "Christians" and taking the Bible as their only rule of faith, had advocated a Christian union. This movement had grown out of the Great Revival which, reaching its height about 1805, had encouraged a younger and more democratic element in the Presbyterian Church to preach a modified Calvinism. This divisive tendency developed easily into a schism in the Presbyterian Church. One minister was tried by the Synod of Kentucky and was found guilty of preaching anti-Calvinistic doctrines. Four other revival preachers, protesting against the action of the synod, withdrew from its jurisdiction and created a new organization which for a while was generally called the Christian Church. In the new sect the dominant idea of absolute freedom in worship destroyed any plan for union with other denominations. Separate and independent, the leaders lost their purpose within a few years. Of the five who had seceded, two joined the Shakers and two returned to the Presbyterian fold. The fifth, Barton W. Stone, spent the remainder of his life in independent evangelical work and in organizing churches in Tennessee, Kentucky, Ohio, Indiana, and Illinois.

Throughout most of his life Stone faced the problem of earning a living for himself and his family from some source other than that of the church. In 1812 he moved to the Mansker Creek settlement in middle Tennessee. Unhappy there and unable to carry on his church work, he returned to Kentucky in 1815. While teaching a school in Lexington and later in Georgetown, he bought a farm in 1819 on the North Elkhorn River, a mile from Georgetown. By now he was looked on as something of a patriarch among devotees to a movement that antedated by several years the reforming efforts of Thomas and Alexander Campbell. Naturally Stone, with a Presbyterian background, hesitated to accept the teachings of Alexander

Campbell concerning free will, original sin, and total depravity.

In an effort to make known his own views and to disseminate information about the Stoneites or Christians, Stone began in November, 1826, the publication of a monthly paper, the *Christian Messenger*. First published at Georgetown, Kentucky, and later at Jacksonville, Illinois, the *Messenger* appeared as a twenty-four-page pamphlet with some intermissions until 1845, a year after the death of Stone. With few subscribers even at a subscription rate of one dollar a year, the paper, despite its tenuous existence, became a valuable medium of expression. Some issues contained items which interested readers besides those of the Stone persuasion. Although published in a slave state until Stone moved to Illinois in 1834, the *Messenger* steadfastly gave voice to antislavery sentiment. Sometimes the paper drew violent criticisms attended by a loss of subscriptions.

In 1824 Barton Stone met Alexander Campbell and at once was aware of the spiritual attraction between them. Granting that he was not in complete accord with some of Campbell's views, Stone was a willing partner to an agreement in 1832 whereby Christians and Disciples would act as one in a loose union. By this time the Campbellites and the Stoneites, exceedingly attractive to people who had become dissatisfied with the denominational divisions, had about twenty thousand members. Both groups desired a union of all Christians, rejected creeds, rejected limited atonement, and recognized the ability of the individual to understand and accept the evidence of Christ. In several aspects there were differences. The Campbell group insisted on plenary immersion as a condition of church membership; Stone had misgivings about the requirement but positively believed in baptism for the remission of sins. Both groups had repudiated the authority of presbyteries and synods, but Campbell's followers had retained a great fear of the ministerial hierarchy. Campbell had little respect for conversions made in the Methodist type of revivalism which had been adopted by the Stoneites and preferred to win his adherents through a reasonable approach. To be specific, Campbell preferred to persuade, to proselyte, to convince men that they should leave one church and join another. Stone, in contrast to Campbell, did not require the weekly observance of the Lord's Supper or the practice of close communion.

In the long run the points of agreement far outweighed those of disagreement. Each group had simplified its beliefs until a proposed union was feasible and sensible. Stone provided the sane, judicious, gentle, and gracious side of the nebulous partnership. He recognized the strong leadership of Campbell and, deeming the egotism of Campbell a needed adjunct, gave him control of the now aggressive movement. Since complete union was never attained, two distinct groups used the nomenclature "Christian Church." The larger group, arising from the Campbell-Stone union, is usually designated as the Disciples of Christ, and the smaller group is known as the Christian Church or Christian Connexion. In this effort to return to the simplicity of the early Christian church there was nothing new or radical. Many people through the centuries had sought the restoration of apostolic ordinances, and others have followed them with no more success. It is one of the ironies of history that all movements which have promised to restore unity in religion have eventually become denominations.

With competition already rife among religious bodies in mid-America, the presence of a new participant was not welcomed by the older organizations. In denominational contests, as in all games, sustained excitement reaches a peak and then subsides to run through quieter channels. Churches that had eyed each other as enemies discovered their strong dislikes had cooled almost to a point of congeniality. Resting in their own stability, the established denominations were ready to pounce on any intruder and to resist the encroachments of the come-lately Disciples of Christ, a sect spawned in the West. Now bound loosely together in a front against the increasing followers of Alexander Campbell, the Presbyterians, Methodists, and Baptists made their attacks on Campbell, whose pronounced opposition to ecclesiastical authority had aroused both fear and resentment among them. Much of the antagonism to the rapidly increasing Disciples can be laid squarely at the feet of Campbell. His harsh attacks on other churches, his pamphleteering crusades, his ceaseless debating, his contending and championing caused other groups to resent the new movement and to combine their resistance against him as the leader of the new sect. John Taylor, a highly respected Baptist leader in Kentucky who obviously had had verbal encounters with Campbell, has described his relationships with people: "The man who would have Campbell as his warm friend, must remember two things; he must be both fool and hypocrite, before friendship can be gained. Two other things are needful, to keep up the friendship, to wit: flattery and submission."

As the underlying factor in his reformation, Campbell laid emphasis on "The Restoration of the Ancient Order of Things," a phrase which to him meant the achievement of Christian union without creed and beyond sectarianism. For a few years he sought his goal so vigorously and belligerently that he almost destroyed his plan for union. In his enthusiasm for union, he was so all-embracing that he came near to accepting such practices as foot washing which had brought extinction or obscurity to some branches of the Baptists. From platform and press he opposed, almost with fanaticism, some organizations sponsored or supported by other denominations. He loudly denounced Bible, tract, and missionary societies, and said that Sunday schools were "recruiting establishments" designed "to fill up the ranks of those sects which take the lead in them." He assumed a position of infallibility, making such pronouncements as: "I take the Bible for my sole guide. I cannot possibly be wrong in any particular. None but myself (and my disciples) take the Bible as their guide. Wherever they differ from me, they differ from the Bible."

Having, so to speak, the inside track on Biblical interpretation, Campbell asserted and reasserted his unique position. He proclaimed every baptized person, however ignorant, to be a preacher and scoffed at theological schools and a paid ministry. Nathan L. Rice, a Presbyterian leader and a hostile critic of many people, charged that Campbell attacked and slandered all Protestant ministers, throwing them together as "a venal set of men, actuated by the most sordid motives." By steady repetition Campbell hypnotized his followers and irritated his opponents to the point that the latter met him in frenzy. Such an opponent was Joseph C. Stiles, a Presbyterian minister in Kentucky, who in writing to Campbell revealed his extreme exasperation: "The reader of your works would sometimes imagine that your head was a great storehouse of theological quibbles. You seem to have studied out and treasured up every thing that could be said against every text and argument which stands for the truth; and every ingenious gloss and sophism that promises currency to error."

At the outset of a personal encounter, Campbell usually had a decided advantage over his adversary: good bearing, self-assurance, ready tongue, quick pen, clever repartee, critical acumen—all provided him with excellent equipment for any battle of words. Although not a great scholar, Campbell used in his sermons and lectures a style that suggested vast knowledge and deep resources. Much that was old and commonplace often appeared as new and original when written or spoken by him. He was adept at twisting the meaning of words to suit his need. Many of his opponents were of the opinion that often he placed an unwarranted emphasis on statements or quotations in an effort to confound them. He was ever ready and willing to debate an issue. His frequent appearance in public debates allowed Campbell to publicize his own opinion and to disparage the views of his opponents.

In public encounters he ranged over a wide variety of topics and met with an assortment of men. He debated with John Walker, a Seceder minister in Ohio, and with William L. MacCalla, a Presbyterian minister in Kentucky, on baptism; with Abner Kneeland, a Universalist clergyman, on atheism; with Robert Owen, the utopian socialist, on religious skepticism; and with John Purcell, the Catholic bishop of Cincinnati, on Romanism. Campbell probably reached the pinnacle of his forensic fame early in his career in a debate with Robert Owen. For ten days in 1829, before great crowds in Cincinnati, he brilliantly defended Christianity against the champion of skepticism.

His techniques caused some men of good reputation to consider Campbell an unfair debater. The fear of proving a poor opponent influenced many able clergymen to decline Campbell's offer to meet in debate over theological questions. And some would have willingly accepted the loss of face had they thought the verbal encounters would have had any value. Thomas Cleland wrote: "I have no wish to enter the arena of controversy with such a man. I should gain nothing but certain defeat; sharing the same fate of . . . all other writers of the brotherhood." Continuing in his criticism of Campbell, Cleland spared no punches: "As to truth and candor, meekness and charity, fair reasoning and manly argument, these belong not to his escutcheon. But empty declamation, flashes of abortive wit and ridicule, horrific apostrophising, tripping levity and irony, quibbling on single words and punning on letters in the alphabet, immodest pretensions to superior talents; these, and such like, form the missiles of this modern Golia[t]h. . . ." Gideon Blackburn, a Presbyterian minister of Louisville, also let Campbell's challenge for a meeting go unaccepted.

A few colleagues and supporters of Campbell dared to speak out that they thought he was too unrelenting in his attacks on other denominations. In 1827 Stone expressed such an admonition to his associate, "We confess our fear that in some of your well-intended aims at error you have unintentionally wounded the truth." Robert B. Semple, a Baptist preacher in Virginia, wrote in 1827 to a correspondent in Kentucky that he hoped Campbell "will be brought to a more scriptural and more rational course." Although Henry Ward Beecher was highly sympathetic with Campbell's "great work for the union of Christians and their emancipation from the thralldom of creeds and priestcraft," he feared that Campbell was unconsciously going in the wrong direction. He observed among Campbell's followers "a strong tendency to literalism—to a scrupulous devotion to the letter of the law, rather than to the spirit of the Book." This literalism Beecher believed was a hindrance to public acceptance of Campbell's theology and constituted a dangerous deterrent to the general reception of other doctrines.

Early in the course of his crusade Campbell became aware of the great value in a continuing medium by which his reforms could be promulgated, his opinions disseminated, and his criticisms of the Baptists broadcast. For this purpose he established in 1823 at his home in Bethany, Virginia, a small monthly magazine, the *Christian Baptist*. Having moved to Bethany in 1811, Campbell lived out his long life there in comfort on several hundred acres of good land, a gift from his prosperous father-in-law. The village gained notoriety as the location of Campbell's publications, and in time the place-name became, for all practical uses, synonymous with that of the editor. In 1830 as evidence of wider interest in world evangelization, Campbell discontinued his first magazine and began publishing the *Millennial Harbinger*. As the name of the paper indicated, Campbell had been affected by a delusion of an immediate Second Coming of Christ. With some shifting of emphases the *Harbinger* continued publication until 1870. The output of Campbell's press was so large that the federal government established a post office at Bethany and made him the postmaster, a position which he held for thirty years.

Through the media of these two magazines Campbell extended the fields of his attack far beyond the range of his oral debates. Sparing neither sarcasm nor irony, he wrote with a harshness that pleased his followers and smarted his opponents. In the name of Christianity he unleashed a flood of epithets and personal attacks and excused these features on the basis that he must be given a hearing. Eagerly his friends and adversaries awaited the next issues in order to learn on whom Campbell had turned his volleys. The two magazines had a wide circulation in Virginia where the educated and cultured people with slaves had time to read and to write. In the newer communities with less leisure there were fewer subscribers.

Among the Baptist leaders and editors Campbell left few untouched. Careless with personal remarks, he often lost his judgment in acid invectives. In 1834 he described the style of Robert B. C. Howell as being "more like that of Pope Leo X, than of a Christian preacher." He further charged that Howell had resorted to falsehoods in an article and had preached sermons which were filled with plagiarisms from Campbell's debates. If one considers the erudition and ability of Howell as a pulpit orator and as the editor of *The Baptist,* Campbell's accusation raises an eyebrow.

Toward many of his Baptist opponents time did not mellow the approaches of Campbell. As late as 1853 he, somewhat justifiably, used little if any restraint in describing James R. Graves, editor of the *Tennessee Baptist*:

"I have known a few men in my life who made themselves simpletons, in attempting to act as knaves. Mr. Graves certainly has kept bad company, else he does himself great injustice." A few months later in a biting editorial Campbell wrote that the *Tennessee Baptist* was "surcharged with venom and falsehood" and that Graves was "either the most stupid, or the most reckless of truth, of any sectarian editor" in the country. Three years later Campbell was still hounding Graves, saying that he was "as a monument of that class of preachers and editors who have for years been opposing, misrepresenting, and slandering us and the cause we plead."

Needless to say, the alert and acidulous Baptist editors did not read in silence; they contributed their share to the verbal religious war. In 1846 the *Western Baptist Review* noted that Campbell had at last published his creed. The editor regretted that it had not been published earlier and thereby saved a lot of misunderstanding and discussion. Exulting in victory, he wrote: "The conflict then is over, and peace restored on the subject. The skull of the great champion *vs.* creeds is broken by a pebble from his own beach: he is decapitated by his own sword." These are patently the words of a wishful Baptist, for Campbell at no time acknowledged defeat.

Since the Baptist and the Methodist churches suffered the greatest losses to the Disciples, some statistics of membership in the State of Kentucky will bear sufficient evidence of the proselyting activities of the early Disciples.

The Green River Association of Baptists fell from 2,951 members in 1830 to 740 in 1832. The Elkhorn, the largest association in the state, had 4,488 in 1829 and 3,277 in 1836. Between 1829 and 1839 the Franklin Association dropped in membership from 1,860 to 1,484. The Kentucky Conference of the Methodist Episcopal Church, founded in 1820, counted 23,723 members in the fall of 1821. By 1826 the membership had fallen to 20,492, but had increased to 26,193 in 1832. Within eleven years the conference had gained only 2,470 members. During the same period the number of Methodists in the United States increased from 297,622 to 599,736. Reports from other states show evidence hardly as marked as that in Kentucky of the losses sustained by these two major churches in the South.

Because a large number of the people who had early associated themselves with the Disciples were proselyted from Baptist, Methodist, and Presbyterian churches, strong antagonisms to the new sect readily developed in these denominations. The Baptists, whose losses in members were significant, naturally became leaders in the attacks on the Disciples which lasted until the Roman Catholics seemed a greater threat than the Disciples. The battle continued in the press, in the pulpit, under the trees—anywhere a reader or hearer might be found. Sometimes the contest was conducted on a high plane and too frequently on a low level. A certain Baptist must have been exasperated to the breaking point when, calling himself "A

Subscriber," he wrote a violent attack on Campbell in 1830 and sent it to the editor of a Baptist paper. Piling abuse upon abuse, he concluded his tirade on Campbell with further immoderation: "If I had evidence of his being a Christian, I should call him a spiritual B——d; but that name is not appropriate. There is not a meeting-house except those of the Universalists or Unitarians that will admit him into their pulpits." In the early 1830's the Franklin Baptist Association in Kentucky issued a Circular Letter deploring the disappearance of harmony, peace, the one gospel, the one faith, and its replacement by "the fell spirit of discord [which] stalks in open day through families, neighborhoods and churches."

Campbell's boldest attacks on the Baptists had come at a vulnerable time when Baptist churches were being torn by the antimissionary fight and the question of pastoral support. William Vaughan, a Western Baptist preacher of moderately judicious temperament, felt that Campbell's success was due in a large measure to the ambiguity of his position and to his ability to befog issues. As a result, so he said, Campbellism grew, expanded, and "raged like an epidemic in many parts of the country," dividing and wrecking churches at random.

Some attempts to thwart the Disciples were childlike and ludicrous. Having hauled two loads of planks to be used as seats at a meeting in Kentucky, the Disciples returned to the church lot on Sunday and found all the benches were burned. Public rumor placed the blame on the Baptists, Presbyterians, and Methodists, all of whom remained suspiciously silent. In order to prevent a large attendance at a Disciple meeting in Franklin, Tennessee, in 1833 the Baptist and Methodist churches arranged for meetings on the same days as those chosen by the Disciples. In 1837 in Tuscaloosa, Alabama, a Baptist musician with "his boisterous minstrels" so successfully sang down the Disciples that they were forced to wait until after twelve o'clock to start a sermon.

Because of the adeptness with which the Disciples proselyted the Baptists in many areas, several Baptist associations passed resolutions against the Disciples. In 1830 the South District Association in Kentucky resolved to advise her churches to disapprove the writings of Campbell and those preachers who propagate his destructive sentiments. The Mississippi Association declared it would not fellowship or commune with anyone holding the doctrines or dogmas of "the christian Baptists, *alias,* the Campbellites." In 1831 a Baptist group in Illinois calling themselves The Friends to Humanity Association issued a circular letter warning of a prevalent infidelity which "has assumed a thousand forms such as deism, atheism, Campbellism, Mormonism, Parkerism, and drunkenness." In describing the effects of Campbellism on the South Elkhorn (Kentucky) Baptist Church, a correspondent in 1838 wrote: "Their boasted reformation has proved but a moral pestilence and mildew upon religion in that region. . . . They are religious salamanders, and live only in the fire of strife and contention." Four years later a Baptist correspondent from Louisiana with tongue in cheek observed that some associations were enjoying good health because they had not been "visited by the wonderfully irridiating [*sic*] beams of Campbellism." A pamphlet circulating in Missouri as late as 1858 bore the title, "No Communion with Campbellites," and asked the question, "Are Campbellites converted?"

Such is a sampling of the quarrels and controversies that existed between the Baptists and the Disciples. Campbell's early association with the Baptists had acquainted him with some distinctive features of that denomination with which he wanted no part—some elements of doctrine, the confession of Christian experience before baptism, and the use of creeds and confessions of faith. The Baptists had indeed pursued policies that provided a perfect ground for the launching of the Disciples of Christ. Albert H. Newman, an able historian of the Baptists in America, has analyzed the situation within the Baptist churches that permitted the growth of a new sect. Laying responsibility on the Baptists for their own disruption, Newman arraigned them for the lack of a better educated clergy, a wider missionary program, and a more evangelical doctrine. Had the Baptists followed a more intelligent course, he says, no movement such as that one led by Campbell could have possibly arisen, gained a following, and developed into a new sect.

Since Campbellism was also an ever present threat to

the membership of the Methodist Church, many Methodist preachers and revivalists adopted a policy of criticizing and ridiculing Campbell and his followers just as the Baptists did. Always on the outlook for an opponent of Methodism, Peter Cartwright dubbed Campbell as the "giant errorist" who had misled Stone in his old age to form a union of Christians and Disciples. Cartwright criticized the failure of the Christians to provide at the Cane Ridge Revival in 1801 ministers who were "settled in Gospel doctrine and Church discipline." As a result of this failure, thousands who could have been saved "finally made shipwreck of the faith, fell back, turned infidel, and lost their religion and their souls forever." Cartwright was sure that "fishing in the muddy waters of Campbellism" had led a Kentucky Baptist preacher, whom he described as "a pretty clever, intelligent old gentleman," to lose his mental balance. He speciously alleged that Campbellite preachers involved the Methodists in "vain and hurtful debates," in order "to confuse the minds of the people, and draw them off from seeking God." At a camp meeting in Illinois in 1843 Cartwright came to the defense of a Methodist who was being provoked into a debate by a Disciple preacher. He felt very sure that he had "silenced his batteries" by saying to the offender, "Now sir, . . . if you think [you are able] to provoke me to condescend to turn aside from carrying on this glorious work to debate with you, the evil spirit that prompts you does but deceive you; for it seems to me it would be like loading a fifty-six to kill a fly. . . ."

Here and there the Methodists lost members to the Disciples because of the latter's great emphasis on immersion as a mode of baptism. In order to meet this challenge, some Methodist preachers on occasion departed from their usual custom of sprinkling and used plenary immersion. Only an acute situation in Fayette, Missouri, could have driven William W. Redman, a Methodist preacher "in high standing," to immerse six adults while the presiding elder stood on the bank with "looks and exclamations of considerable disapprobation." The Methodists, casting aspersions freely, criticized the morals of the Disciples and their religious views. One writer, noting the wide range of Methodist criticism, concluded that "with the help of the Devil, [Methodists] would lead men on until they accomplished their own damnation." Tolbert Fanning, a Disciple preacher and teacher of wide reputation in Tennessee, made a Southern tour in 1847 and evidently gave stiff competition to the Methodists in Alabama. Seeking to combat this newcomer, the Methodists claimed that Fanning had become "prostrated in a straw pen, [and] made a public confession of religion" at Cypress Camp Ground in Lauderdale County. Fanning denied this charge and its implications and countercharged that the Methodists had kept up a "continual sluice of misrepresentation" against his church and his own Franklin College in Nashville.

Observing the animosity among the Methodists in Memphis, B. F. Hall, a Disciple minister, wrote in 1851: "The Methodists are preaching against us at a terrible rate; call my name in the pulpit, ridicule our sentiments; say everything they can, low and hard." Hall's keen awareness of the situation is revealed in his next terse and correct statement: "We laugh at them, and keep baptizing their members."

William Phillips, a Methodist preacher in Kentucky, published a brief doggerel poem entitled "Alexander the Great; or, The Learned Camel." Copies were circulated by the thousands, probably to the amusement of Campbell and his followers. The publicity, as usual, was turned to an advantage by the Disciples. The notoriety that the poem brought to Phillips may have contributed to his appointment as assistant editor of the *Western Christian Advocate* of Cincinnati. Fountain E. Pitts, a considerable force in Methodist circles in Tennessee, was highly critical of Alexander Campbell and his movement. In a small book, *Tracts on Campbellism,* Pitts called Campbell "one of the most hypercritical sophists of the age" who was seeking to immortalize his name. Pitts charged that the crusade "under the imposing insignia of a *reformation* is a *humbug*," and that in the pursuit of union the Disciples of Christ had attempted to capitalize on the differences among the various churches.

Through their church papers the Methodists, as if bound by an understanding with Baptist and Presbyterian papers, attacked Campbell on a variety of counts. On most occasions he was equal to the opposition, for he had a private press to serve as a vehicle for his ceaseless writing. In 1843 Campbell announced that the various Methodist *Advocates* had poured on him "the unmitigated vials of their holy indignation." He then proceeded to belittle the Methodist minister, saying he was a "storming declaimer, who rubs his inspiration out of his hands, who converts by a stentorian pitch of voice, who . . . can knock a sinner down with the fist of holiness, or whip him into the fold with the scourge of righteousness. . . ." Campbell admitted that, in a degree, this type of preaching used by the Methodists was successful because "nine-tenths of mankind . . . admire those who praise the whirlwind and rejoice in the storm." He asserted that the Methodists were so eager for members that anyone who beats his breast or says he is a sinner is admitted "within the pale of the Methodist sanctuary." When Campbell was asked to whom he would send an inquirer concerning primitive Christianity, in reply he showed his contempt for Methodism, saying he would refer the seeker to a "devout Mussulman" rather than to a Methodist circuit rider or to a Methodist journal.

Against the religious excitement in which the Methodists indulged, Campbell directed some of his harshest blows. Many of the Methodist efforts, he insisted, were "the mere offspring of excited feelings—of sympathy with tones, and attitudes, and gestures—of the noise, and tumult, and shoutings. . . ." He nursed a grave doubt that revivals had been an advantage to true and vital religion. In an editorial Campbell assailed the Methodist class meeting as an "institution in opposition to the proclamation of mercy, not only destitute of scriptural precept or precedent, but at variance with both the letter and spirit of Christianity." He called the anxious seat "one of the most dangerous and delusive inventions" which was "too gross for intelligent men of much spirituality." He was of the opinion that the Methodists were responsible for the prevailing lack of reverence for the Bible because they were guilty of an "irrational reliance upon noise, passion, and animal feeling."

Not content with reaching people only by his papers and pamphlets, Campbell traveled thousands of miles in the Midwestern section of the country. He thrived on expeditions into enemy territory. His tours took him over so much of the country that he became one of the best known men in America. His activities in Tennessee are typical of any place at any time. In December, 1830, he was in Franklin "among the icebergs of Calvinism," as he said. From there he went to Columbia, preached and, in a baptismal ceremony, immersed three persons in the chilling waters of Duck River. On Christmas Day he was in Nashville debating with Obadiah Jennings, minister of the leading Presbyterian church in the town. In the debate Jennings pointed his arguments on Campbell's efforts to divide the church rather than to unite Christians. This subject was a vulnerable point concerning which Campbell later had to justify the direction of his efforts. When Jennings' partisans presented him with a suit of clothes, many considered the gift as a token of victory; but on this matter a man on the scene made a different observation, saying that Campbell had converted thirty to his side and Jennings had gained none. Robert Richardson, Campbell's biographer, later accused Jennings of repeating numerous misrepresentations which had been circulated about Campbell.

Recalling Campbell's Presbyterian heritage and his defection, the Presbyterians permitted Campbell no escape from their recriminations. As a denomination with high regard for education and theological training, the Presbyterian Church stood aghast but not speechless at Campbell's acceptance of an untrained lay leadership. Nathan L. Rice, describing these laymen, wrote: "They have but to profess to believe *one fact,* and to be immersed; and without previous study, literary or theological, whether able to read intelligently or not, they at once become teachers of religion. . . . And those who possess some smartness and fluency, may hope to be chosen by the little independent church to the high and important office of bishop! Is it wonderful that great numbers of ambitious persons, who could become distinguished in no other church, should hasten to this?" In indignation Rice shows his extreme Presbyterian position as he gasps over the ignorant preachers assuming the role of censors of trained theologians: "Boys in their *teens,* or youths who, for years to come, would not have been permitted to lay a shoulder of mutton on God's ancient altar, are now gravely and learnedly exposing the errors of Luther, Calvin, Wesley, the Synods of Dort, Westminster, and Trent. . . ." The Philadelphia *Presbyterian* recognized Campbell as a well known and influential figure in the Western country, but the editors were of the opinion that "few living errorists have done so much to rend and corrupt the church in that region" as had Campbell. Although the tension with Presbyterians lessened and the fire dimmed with the passage of years, as late as 1845 a Presbyterian minister in Alabama dared to describe the Disciples as being the "very fag end of Creation" because they were the refuse excluded from Baptist, Methodist, and Presbyterian churches.

The antagonism toward the Disciples spread from preacher and editor to lay leaders and occasionally infected entire communities. So too, jealousy flared up in regions far removed from the centers of Disciple activities. Around Natchez and Woodville, Mississippi, Jacob Creath, Jr., verging on a break with the Baptists in favor of Campbellism, aroused such violent opposition to his preaching that he was burned in effigy. A friend warned him that his life was in danger and that he had narrowly escaped hanging. Several years later opposition still ran high in Holmes County where the people and the churches resented the new movement. There they were called Campbellites and infidels. As late as 1854 John T. Johnson, a Disciple preacher from Kentucky, spent fifteen days in and near Woodville and found strong sectarian opposition there. Although politely treated by the citizens, Johnson found no welcome from the preachers, none of whom "poked his head out of his den. . . ."

From Texas came similar reports. In the spring of 1841, J. P. Marshall moved from Kentucky to Texas where he was an active preacher for the Disciples. Two years later Marshall stated that he could write a volume on the opposition he had met from the Methodists, Presbyterians, and particularly the Baptists, who were "more exceedingly virulent than all the others." He found the Methodists a great nuisance with their interruptions of his sermons in order to present contradictions. In 1839 J. A. Clark had likewise gone from Kentucky to Texas, practiced law for a period, and then established a school. Resenting his conversion to Campbellism, some of his patrons demanded that he surrender the title to the school property and close the school. The prejudices against Clark increased so far that his effectiveness as a teacher was ruined and he was forced to cease teaching.

In several counties in Alabama, Disciples and Christians met stiff opposition from a variety of preachers and laymen of several denominations. Almost without exception congregations refused to extend the use of their buildings for services. Commenting on such discourtesy in Mooresville, a Disciple knowingly observed: "It is very presumptuous in these Cumberland [Presbyterians] to behave so. They have just been gasping for breath all their lives. . . ."

One reformer visiting in Alabama wrote of "the most virulent opposition" which came from the "refined class

of mankind, these nobles of belligerent sectarianism."
Sorely he had felt the barbs from "these lords of Christian-
ized factions" who regarded as "odious, hateful, despicable,
those who advocate primitive and apostolic christianity."
Certainly, he had felt no warmth of welcome in south
Alabama. But there can be no doubt that the advocates of
primitive Christianity were achieving a reformation in
many places. In Chambers and Russell counties some
one hundred members resolved to free themselves from the
"shackles of sectarianism," namely, that of the Baptists,
and withdrew in 1845 from two Baptist churches in the
counties. This action disturbed the Methodists and Presbyterians, and they banded with the Baptists to face the on-
slaught of the Disciples.

When the Disciples took no outspoken position for or
against slavery, the people in the South particularly were
puzzled by the silence and inferred that persons without
avowed opinions must be abolitionists. In Lowndes County,
Alabama, James A. Butler, the only Disciple preacher
in the state in 1835, was arrested on some flimsy charge
regarding abolitionism and was threatened with bodily
harm. Leaving the county, Butler settled in Tuscaloosa
where, with the aid of Alexander Graham, he published a
monthly paper. Working under adverse conditions and
amid criticisms, the editors were able to publish *The Disciple* for only two years.

Only on the question of slavery did Campbell and his
reformers escape persistent attacks. The leaders and mem-

bers of opposing churches were somewhat doubtful about
Campbell's position on this national issue. Holding to "the
ancient order of things," Campbell recognized the relation
of master and slave as not immoral, since it had Biblical
status. In the absence of any pyramidal form of church
government, no pronouncements, edicts, rulings, or resolutions disturbed the congregations of Disciples. There was
no rule of the majority to strengthen or alter the opinion
of the individual. Numerous churches of Methodist, Baptist, and Presbyterian denominations, having been torn by
schisms and permanent divisions, looked enviously at the
isolated security which each Disciple congregation enjoyed. The Disciples like the Episcopalians relied on their
basic element of Christian unity to keep them removed
from sectional and temporal disruptions. "We are," said
Campbell, "the only religious community in the civilized
world whose principles (unless we abandon them) can preserve us from such an unfortunate predicament."

If any group was justified in questioning Campbell's
attitudes toward the slavery issue, it was his own followers,
for Campbell had given evidence of shifting positions when
he looked the institution of slavery squarely in the face.
In 1829 he had successfully sought election to the Virginia
Constitutional Convention as an antislavery leader. At this
time he was very critical of slavery and desired to have it
eliminated. In 1832 he went so far as to describe slavery as
"that largest and blackest blot upon our national escutcheon." By 1845 he had arrived at the conclusion that slavery

was not unchristian, and he placed his sympathy with the owners of slaves rather than with the slaves. When challenged as vacillating with regard to slavery—and he was, for many denounced him as proslavery in attitude, others as antislavery, and some as abolitionist—Campbell said his position had been fashioned by "expediency" in order to guarantee unity to his church. When facing accusations of being an abolitionist, Campbell replied, "I have always been anti-slavery, but never an abolitionist. . . ." In order to clarify his views on slavery, Campbell in 1845 wrote a series of eight articles for the *Millennial Harbinger* on "Our Position to American Slavery." In answer to communications he provided a good summary of the series: "I have endeavored to show how Christians should act in the present crisis . . . and not how *Abolitionists or Pro-Slavery Men* should act in their political schemes. I am neither the one nor the other. I am neither the advocate nor the apologist of American or any other kind of slavery."

Probably because of the small membership in the Protestant Episcopal Church and his few contacts with its laity and clergy, Campbell rarely mentions the Episcopalians in writing or lecturing. Campbell did see fit to criticize Philander Chase, Bishop of the Episcopal Church in Ohio, for buying patens, chalices, and plates after he had toured England soliciting twenty thousand dollars. The simplicity of the altars in the Disciple churches required no elaborate equipment and the presence of such indicated only needless extravagance. A warm friendship existed between Campbell and James H. Otey, Bishop of the Episcopal Church in Tennessee, and each had respect for the work of the other. Unaccustomed to complimentary remarks about other churches, subscribers to the *Christian Teacher*, a Disciple paper, had to re-read an article praising the Episcopal Bishop of Kentucky as a leader "magnanimous and correct" in his religious views. The paper saluted Bishop Benjamin B. Smith for his expressed opposition to the "blighting curse of sectarianism." Had the wind changed?

One man cannot say how or why the thinking of another man changes, but modifications can be observed and the new relationships noted. The events of the 1840's and 1850's prompted a regrouping of people, and new sentiments caused new alignments. To what extent these affected the acceptance of Campbell and his Disciples, it is difficult to judge; but the relations eased and softened among Protestant organizations confronted with increasing national disunity and with expanding Catholicism. Campbell, having won for his theology a substantial following, was now less harsh, less egotistical, and less dictatorial. He was moved to accept new programs and reversed his earlier hostile attitude toward missions, Sunday schools, and other agencies which had been employed so effectively by other churches. He had established himself as a gifted leader of a new church born in the very midst of the competitive denominational struggle in the Midwest; and his opponents, seeing him with familiarity and new perception,

found less in him to fear and more to like. When invited
to preach in November, 1854, in the Methodist Church in
Nashville, Campbell spoke to "a densely crowded audience." One of his hearers remarked that the discourse
showed "the genius and *talents*" of the noted visitor. The
suspicions about Campbell were gradually fading among
his opponents. For at least a quarter of a century the founders of the Disciples of Christ, trained and hardened in the
West, had beaten back every major challenge and resistance of the older denominations. Eventually the newcomer
was recognized not as a radical innovator but as a product
of modified Presbyterianism coupled with selected Baptist
practices. Even the Baptists, who earlier had had so much
reason to distrust and to challenge Campbell at every step,
grudgingly accepted him and his reformation. It was indeed a wise old Baptist preacher who advised his congregation that "the best way to fight Campbellism is to let it
alone." His wisdom went further, however, as he looked at
his own church: "We have more to fear from our own
preachers and members—from their imprudences and mis-
conduct—than from our enemies."

The West was admirably suited for the rise and growth
of this new church. Campbell was always aware of the great
vantage ground within which his followers sought to convince and to convert. The simplicity of his gospel, freed
from the subtleties of Calvinism and preached by a native-
born lay group, had powerful appeal and bore significant
results. By 1860 this denomination had some 200,000 mem-

bers. Together Stone and Campbell had built a church that has been aptly described as "an example of a religious movement true to the genius of the democratic peoples of America, riding the wave of westward expansion and becoming a voice and vehicle of the religious aspirations."

The Disciples of Christ, as a well constituted, ably led, enthusiastically supported, and generally accepted denomination, added much to Protestant strength in the West and the South. When conditions are reversed, the oppressed often becomes a powerful oppressor. Once the Disciples had moved from the status of a sect to that of a denomination, they forthwith became an ally with other anti-Catholic churches. Old animosities were forgotten, new bases for fellowships were found, and common ground for cooperation was established in order to build a coalition against the Catholics.

III

PROTESTANTS AGAINST CATHOLICS

WHEN LYMAN BEECHER ACCEPTED IN 1832 THE presidency of Lane Seminary in Cincinnati, he not only assumed the management of this recently founded theological school of the Presbyterian Church but also accepted the challenge to stand firm against Roman Catholicism and to prevent the Pope from extending his influence to the vast Mississippi Valley. In a powerful and inflaming sermon Beecher presented his case for Protestantism; and, when the sermon was published three years later under the title *A Plea for the West,* he widened his reach, stirring many Protestants to anger and some to activity. Other sermons and other books reiterated the responsibilities which faced Protestantism; but none painted so dark a picture as did Horace Bushnell's book *Barbarism the First Danger,* in which the author declared Romanism to be the great threat to the West, second only to ignorance and illiteracy. Theocrats like Beecher and Bushnell assisted greatly in popularizing Samuel F. B. Morse's *Foreign Conspiracy against the Liberties of the United States.* Morse's book, published in 1835, supplied the fire for most of the anti-Catholic literature of the next decade, and flame throwing became a popular diversion in this period of American history. Since no conspiracy really existed outside of Morse's mind or book, it is difficult to explain his "disclosures." Regardless of the motivation, Morse gave his view of the political principles of Catholicism and urged Protestants to defend their own republican ideas.

The opposition to Roman Catholicism was more historical than doctrinal. The early settlers in the American colonies came from an English background of intolerance and hatred of the Papacy. Although the new land, theoretically, should have encouraged tolerance, there were numerous forces that sustained the bigotry of the older sections. English officials had placed severe restrictions on Catholics, and differences were small between the privileges allowed in the colonies and those in England during the seventeenth century. Only in Maryland did the Catholics receive a welcome in the American colonies. During the French and Indian War anti-Catholic bitterness flared but soon died down when the French surrendered their claims to the Ohio Valley. The political leaders of the American Revolution accepted religious tolerance and liberties as fundamentals in American democracy, and at least for a period around the Revolution good relations existed between Catholics and Protestants.

Since Catholics were so few in the country, they were generally regarded as constituting no danger. Respect for the Catholic Church tended to increase in the early years of the new century because of the fine caliber of French priests who sought refuge from war-torn Europe. These were men of deep spirituality, infinite charm, good breeding, and much learning. Undoubtedly, these priests contributed a great deal to the maintenance of a brief era free from discrimination. In this period the Catholic Church in America was "probably more socially acceptable than ever again in its history." Revivalism, which involved most of the Western Protestants, also brought a dormant period of antagonism to Catholics, but the peaceful interludes were not of long duration.

By the 1820's and the 1830's conditions for a Protestant campaign against Catholics were yearly growing more opportune. The Cumberland Schism had grown into a denominational breach, and the Cumberland Presbyterian Church gained recognition for itself from the parent Presbyterian Church and from other denominations. Following a long and bitter period of establishing separate identity, the Disciples of Christ had won a toehold among the Protestant groups. When the Disciples at last were accepted as a new denomination, the older Protestant churches in the South and the Southwest faced no significant defecting group. Since they regarded the Universalists who had some converts beyond the centers of population as being too peculiar to count, the Protestant churches found themselves with no worthy adversary before their united front. While casting about for some mutual opponent, Protestants took a closer look at Catholics, who were indeed a minority group in the West but elsewhere in the United States were considered a threat to Protestant supremacy. Anti-Catholic sentiment was already flourishing in the East, and the ease with which it was transferred to the West was surprising and encouraging.

In this skirmish even the newcomers—Cumberland Presbyterians and Disciples of Christ—entered with about as much enthusiasm as did the Baptists, Presbyterians, and Methodists. The church presses began to plead for missionaries and Bibles for the West in order to prevent the Roman Catholics from instituting there "a system of ignorance, priestcraft, and superstition." Viewing the French Revolution of 1830 as an attack on Papal despotism in Europe, Protestants feared that the time was ripe for a transfer of Catholic power to America. The action of the American Bible Society typifies the counter attack: it urged all Protestants to rise up against "His Holiness, The Pope [who], has, with eager grasp, already fixed upon this fair portion of our Union. . . ." Readily accepting this notion, several other societies quickly and eagerly issued challenging calls for action to save the valley from the alien Catholic.

Beyond question the arrival in America of hordes of Irish immigrants aggravated unpleasant Catholic-Protestant relations and brought festering tempers into rupture. Irish hatred of England was boundless; and, when it was transferred to Congregational New England, the degree of animosity was alarming. Anti-Catholicism in America was never a purely religious sentiment. Social and economic factors brought harsh and recurring conflicts, frightened the natives, and increased the fear that had naturally emanated from a church rooted in foreign soil. In the 1840's the Irish were pouring into the United States at the rate of 100,000 a year. Bringing with them only a few meager possessions, many of the Irish settled in the urban centers of the East and in due time became social problems, touched with all the elements of poverty, slum housing, and unskilled labor. Thus isolated they became the prey of unscrupulous mongers of national prejudices and political movements. Even men whose intellectual achievement and personal integrity should have eradicated ugly prejudices saw the Irish immigrant only as a Catholic threat to Protestant supremacy in America.

Lyman Beecher held the view that three-fourths of the immigrants came from Catholic Europe which furnished them with priests. This combination of church and state, he insisted, made the immigrants as much subjects of European rulers as if they were enlisted in the rulers'

armies. Watching the influx of German and Irish immigrants move into the Ohio Valley, Beecher became increasingly alarmed over the growth of the Catholic population. The Cincinnati diocese reported 50,000 communicants in 1843 and 100,000 three years later, but the church in the area was poor and could serve its members with little more than the sacraments and meager instructions. Fortunately, the immigrants who moved out of the concentration of population along the Atlantic seaboard acquired a positive American spirit more quickly than those who remained in the East. Despite their assimilation into new customs and culture, a foreign air hung over many of the Catholics because of the foreign priests who served the parishes. Like all churches in mid-America, the Catholics were short of native-born clerics and were dependent on those sent from Europe to serve the church in the Western world. As late as 1852 at the First Plenary Council, meeting in Baltimore, only nine of the thirty-two bishops who served dioceses in the United States were native-born.

While New England faced an inundation by the Irish, the Middle West was confronted by a similar threat from the Germans, about one-third of whom were Catholics. Lured by cheap river transportation to the fertile Northwest, the Germans did not drift to the cities, as did the Irish, but set out for the good farm lands where they, even if Catholic in faith, aroused little animosity.

Only the South escaped the full impact of the immigrant

invasion. The Irish avoided the region because of the lack of industrial opportunities; and the Germans, because they did not want to compete with slave labor. Of the fourteen states included in a study of nativism in the South, only Kentucky, Louisiana, Maryland, Missouri, and Texas had enough foreign-born people to create any serious economic, political, and social problems. In Alabama, Virginia, South Carolina, and Tennessee aliens in sizable numbers were found only in the centers of population. The remaining states had a mere handful of the foreign-born.

The Irish put a bold stamp on the Catholic Church in America. Lacking the finesse which had distinguished the old French hierarchy, the Irish priests who were advanced to posts of importance administered their duties with little regard for good public relations in a community. The kind feelings that had earlier existed between Catholics and Protestants in the Mississippi Valley faded with the passing of Father Stephen T. Badin, Father Michael Fournier, and Bishop Joseph B. Flaget. The Irish immigrant had made his church a church of foreigners which grew so rapidly that its three million adherents constituted the largest single denomination in the United States at the opening of the Civil War. Immigration and not the American frontier became the chief factor in the rapid growth and expansion of Catholicism in the West.

As earlier travelers had written about strange sights in the West—Indians, cane, rivers, forests, and grasslands— so the mid-nineteenth century newcomers to Kentucky,

Tennessee, Missouri, and adjacent regions were wont to report on the Catholics who were now in an area that had previously been predominantly Protestant in religion. The reports varied in content; they were rarely congruent; and the same event could be alarming to some and of no consequence to others. Observations and appraisals of the Catholics as a competitive force had one element in common—inconsistency.

Many preachers, visitors, and travelers in the West sent back to their home bases reports of the fearful programs, schemes, and activities of the Catholic Church. Since the center of fear of the Papacy was chiefly in the East, such reports encouraged violent attacks on the church wholly out of keeping with the growth and development of Catholicism in the West. Bishop Samuel Wilberforce of the Anglican Church warned the American Episcopalian, who was without a church in many localities, against the Roman Church, calling it "the enchantress" who, he said, "meets him with her cup of sorcery, and wins him over, whilst there is no other near to whisper to him words of caution, or to shame the fallen Church with open rebuke." Morse was unduly frightened by the amount of missionary aid sent to America by Catholic agencies and societies like the Society for the Propagation of the Faith in France, the Ludwigmissionverein of Munich, and the Leopoldinen Stiftung of Vienna. Bishop John England of the Catholic diocese of Charleston recognized the monetary aid as a source of criticism and doubted the value of the early generosity unless it could be continued in order to meet Protestant antagonisms.

Numerous European observers of the American scene prophesied, as did Frederick Marryat, that "all America west of the Alleghenies will eventually be a Catholic country. . . ." Most commentators who voiced similar opinions based their notions on the multiplicity of Protestant denominations and sects which offered no single, positive religious doctrine. They thought that when the opportunity came to the Westerner to embrace a unified church, he would no longer listen to the exponents of conflicting doctrines. Little did these observers know that for many years the strength of the Protestant churches would come from the spread of sectarianism and the rise of new sects which would appeal to the vast numbers of the unchurched.

The appraisals of all visitors to America were not the same; the observations depended on many variables. Andrew Reed and James Matheson saw little to fear at the hands of the Catholics. These men had been sent to the United States by the Congregational Union of England and Wales in the early 1830's and they had found no Catholic bugbear. They reported that despite the financial support of hundreds of thousands of dollars and a determination to establish itself in the West—the ultimate heart of the country—the Roman Church had fallen behind in the race with other denominations. "Popery cannot flourish in this land," they wrote, "except every thing proper to it should first die out—liberty, conscience, independence, and prejudice. It is not indigenous—it is an exotic; and though fostered by fond hands, and protected by strong ones, it will languish, fade, and fall."

Leaving such vague and indefinite terms as "an exotic religion," "not indigenous," and "multiplicity of sects" to the use of visitors who had come and gone, the Catholics and Protestants on the Western scene recognized each other as competitors and set their harangues at closer aim than any broad terms. The churches became actual participants in namecalling, fought each other with bare hands, and hit hard at many places.

Ignorance was made a weapon: the Catholics used it on the Protestant preachers who knew little about the doctrines of the Catholic Church; and the Protestants aimed it at the Catholic laity who, according to their charges, were kept in total ignorance by the priests. The Catholics were on sure ground when they said the Protestant preachers had no knowledge of the historical background of the church. Fear and hatred had curbed a normal amount of intellectual curiosity; having no point of attack except on the office of the Pope, the Protestants could level their blows on nothing more. In a facetious editorial, "How to Make Up a Lecture against Papacy," the editor of the *Catholic Advocate* (March 22, 1845) listed several ingredients, saying that the quantity mattered little if the whole were capped by a strong tincture of epithets and abusive nicknames. As a last word of caution, he admonished that no trace of scruples should mar the lecture. Rumors had clothed the priests with all sorts of strange ways, and the actual appearance of a priest without one pair of horns disproved the hearsay that he was one of the "outlandish sort of critters." The actual arrival of Bishop England in a Protestant community in Georgia could have been nothing but a disappointing event to the average Georgian who, it was said, "slept on his arms to be continually prepared against treacherous incursions of bloody and faithless Papists banded together for his destruction."

To the Catholic leaders the great variety of Protestants meant religious opportunism and insincerity. Why did some churches recognize the office of bishop and others deny its right of existence? How could it be of divine appointment for some denominations and not for all? What were the functions of the office? So on and on went the comments. While the Baptists were using the Bible to disprove the scriptural foundation of the episcopacy, the Methodists and Episcopalians were quoting the same book for the opposite purpose. One sect could not ordain a minister without the help of a bishop, and others could empower a man to preach when he had had no theological training or any preparation for his task.

The informality of a Protestant service and the style of preaching employed by the minister were other weapons in the Catholic hands. The *Catholic Telegraph* of October 13, 1835, reprinted a report that had appeared in the Brandon (Mississippi) *Register*, which vouched for the authenticity of a sermon preached at Waterproof, Louisiana. The contributor described in realistic details the worst type of Protestant preaching. The preacher, being a Know-Nothing in political leanings and a Hardshell Baptist in religion, was no moderate in the pulpit. Announcing that his text was found somewhere between the first chapter of Genesis and the last one of Revelations, he covered a wide subject repeating often that "he played on a harp uv a thousand strings—spirits uv men made perfeck." The Catholic readers certainly sank back in rectitude as they read of such Protestant polemics. Conditions changed but little in the next ten years, for the *Catholic Advocate* of February 22, 1845, commented on the continued prevailing ignorance among Protestants. "Teach your people to read," an article stated, "and when truth and error grapple, we . . . [shall] have little need to doubt, or to fear, the issue of controversy."

The Roman Catholics met in sharper encounters with the Presbyterians than with any other Protestant denomination. Their clashes were numerous and ranged over the whole doctrinal field; each group, having a well defined theology, could take the offensive and the defensive side as the need arose. Kentucky, a stronghold of both churches, was the scene of the liveliest skirmishes. As debates increased and presses took up the respective causes, strong sentiments got out of control. Some preachers became violently anti-Catholic, as in the case of "the foul mouthed Kirkland" who was barred by the police from street preaching in Louisville. Even Robert J. Breckinridge, a man of good background and a national reputation as a leading Presbyterian, allowed himself to go beyond the bounds of good taste in his attacks on the Catholics. As a rule he centered his most abusive remarks on Mariolatry. He accused the priests of being "the basest and most wicked" of men and branded the laity as "a set of contemptible slaves, crushed by the dank and polluting oppression of their Hierarchy." The editor of the *Catholic Advocate* (September 16, 1837) branded Breckinridge as the "Robespierre of the last [Presbyterian] General Assembly," who unable "to shake one stone in the divine edifice of Catholicity, . . . is determined at least to cover the sacred fabrick all over with filth, in order, if possible, to conceal its divine beauties and proportions. . . ." At a later period the *Advocate* (March 1, 1845) had not increased its regard for the Presbyterian clergy whom it charged with being "the loudest, the most intolerant of all sects, the most tyrannical and ambitious" who wanted "to re-establish by law that holy inquisition, which they can now only infuse into public opinion."

It was not unusual for a Presbyterian preacher, feeling the need for a forensic excursion, to go to Bardstown, Kentucky, the see of the diocese of that name, in order to beard the lion in his den. The activities of the Reverend Nathan Hall illustrate those of other men of like minds. In 1821 Hall made frequent trips to Bardstown, where he made attacks against the Catholics on the street, in a store, or from any pulpit that was empty. On one such trip he learned that Bishop John B. M. David was giving a series of lectures on the Catholic doctrines; it was a ripe moment for Hall who invited Bishop David to meet him in debate at the courthouse. Hall overstepped himself in this encounter; and, since the debate lasted four hours, he had ample opportunity to show how meager was his knowledge of Catholic doctrine. A loud voice in the discussion covered some of the weak points, but when the debates later appeared in pamphlet form Hall proved a poor match for the bishop. Another eager Presbyterian who stepped up too soon to challenge a Catholic speaker was one named Sneed who met Father Francis P. Kenrick in Springfield. Seeing the poor effort made by Sneed, his friends refused to allow him to attempt a rebuttal to Kenrick's masterful presentation. Bishop David observed that Sneed had "vomited all the vermin that he knew about the Catholic church."

There is ample evidence that whole congregations supported the actions of the ministers in their unfriendly attitude toward some denominations. It was the custom of the Presbyterian Church in Louisville to have a parade of children as a part of the Fourth of July celebration. As a rule, the Presbyterians had invited children of other Sunday schools to join them; but in 1836 they purposely excluded the Unitarians, the Roman Catholics, and the Disciples of Christ for the reason that they had no communion with them. Then needing another reason, they claimed that they had a right to invite whom they pleased.

The many denominational papers which flourished in the 1830's provided their readers with accounts of the progress of their own work and the rise and fall of that of their rivals. For most papers it became a regular feature to reprint an article that had appeared elsewhere and for the editor to make biting comments. This habit made each issue the vehicle for a little debate, so to speak. As several Catholic papers were published in the West, they took their place in this paper warfare. The *Catholic Advocate,* published in Bardstown, charged in an issue of March 12, 1836, that the Presbyterian presses had tried for several years to unite all the Protestant papers against the Catholics. The editor admitted that, as he looked over the several exchange copies that came to his desk, he thought the Presbyterians had done a pretty good job. A Presbyterian paper, *Watchman of the South,* true to its name carried a regular feature section entitled "Selections on Popery." As he later perused other papers, the editor of the *Advocate* (May 7, 1836) was pleased to turn from "the disgusting pages" of some Presbyterian papers "burdened with filth and slander" and to find refreshment in "the chaster and more classical columns" of the *American Presbyterian,* published in Nashville by John T. Edgar.

On February 13, 1836, the first issue of the *Western Protestant* was published in Bardstown under the editorship of Nathan L. Rice. The editor stated that the paper had been established primarily as an opponent of the

Catholic Advocate. Truly the editor kept to his purpose, for issue after issue contained anti-Catholic tirades on such topics as penance, baptism, indulgences, and transubstantiation. Rice allowed himself to become involved in the publication of sensational and scurrilous literature. After printing a wild story of an escaped nun who had been seduced by a local priest, Rice faced a suit for defamation of character. Rice lost the case; but his paper lost no subscribers and the editor counted himself the winner after all the unpleasant publicity.

To the Presbyterian one of the most irritating, and probably the least fair, of all Catholic papers published in the West was the *Shepherd of the Valley,* which had been established in St. Louis in 1832. In its barrages it singled out Thomas T. Skillman who edited the *Western Luminary,* a Presbyterian journal published in Kentucky. Quoting Skillman, who had repeatedly warned his readers of their apathy about Romanism, the *Shepherd of the Valley* (February 16, 1833) characterized Skillman as "the conductor of this anti-Catholic hebdomadary" whose "editorial lucubrations" unduly aroused public excitement. The editor's vocabulary no doubt was larger than those of his readers, and with a display of unusual words he seems to add to the mental confusion which he stirred up in each issue of the paper. The tone of his editorials grew increasingly violent, so that finally other Catholics journalists became apologists for his harsh words against the Protestants.

About a decade later the arena for the battle of words shifted to Louisiana. There in a region that had been traditionally and historically Catholic in culture and religion, resentment flared up over the encroachments which the Protestants were making. The *Catholic Sentinel* (January 9, 1845) accused the *New Orleans Protestant,* edited under the auspices of Presbyterians in New Orleans, of publishing gross falsehoods about the Roman Catholics: "This imperious, dictatorial, self-righteous, and eminently libelling *sect* have, since their origin in Geneva, been foremost in the whirlwind of blighting and blasting intolerance." Pointing an accusing finger at the Presbyterians, the editor said they had "slandered, calumniated, and unprovokedly assailed the Roman Catholics of Louisiana. . . ."

The animosity between the Presbyterians and the Catholics also flourished at higher levels than in the local churches. In a strongly worded resolution the Presbyterian General Assembly of 1835 pledged the church "to resist the extension of Romanism." Two years later the Presbyterians divided into the Old School and the New School, almost equal groups distinguished by conservatism and liberalism. The Old School predominated in the South and continued its official policy against the Catholic Church until a decade short of its division in 1861 on a political and geographical basis. The General Assembly of the Old School adopted in 1841 resolutions which were to shape its policy for several years. Pledging a campaign "from the pulpit and through the press, boldly, though temperately, to explain and defend the doctrines and principles of the Reformation, and to point out and expose the errors and superstitions of Popery," the Presbyterians set themselves among the sects opposed to Catholicism. Four years later the assembly debated the validity of Catholic baptism, basing the arguments on whether the Catholic Church was "the true Church of God." When both sides of the question had been tested, the assembly decisively declared that the baptism was invalid and that the priests were but agents of the Pope. In 1849 the assembly adopted resolutions condemning any Protestant parents, church members, or non-church members who sent their children to Romish schools. The assembly denounced any such patronizing as an act "fraught with great danger to their children, and utterly inconsistent with every principle of Protestantism." The action of the assembly in 1852 indicated that political issues had taken precedence over anti-Catholic sentiments. When the Presbytery of Steuben (New Jersey) asked the assembly to recommend that the Presbyterian churches "observe a general concert of prayer to Almighty God, against Romanism," the assembly agreed with the need for supplication on this topic, but deemed "it inexpedient to multiply special occasions of prayer for particular objects."

Here and there among the Presbyterians arose some misgivings about their own anti-Catholic activities. Perhaps they were placing the blame for their own failures on the Catholics; perhaps they had not worked sufficiently hard toward spreading Presbyterianism; perhaps they had attended too much to curbing Catholicism. When a synodical report from Maury County, Tennessee, was made in 1846, the clerk stated that religion in that section was "truly in a languishing condition." A knowing editor of a church paper added his comment to the report: "Have the preachers been neglecting their Zion, in order to abuse the Roman Catholic Church . . . ?"

The Methodists were less violent than the Presbyterians in opposing the Catholics and made no concentrated attacks on them prior to 1844. Since there were few Catholics in the South except in Louisiana and around the centers of population in Kentucky and Missouri, the average Methodist circuit rider rarely ran face to face with one of the papists. But Dame Rumor provided what experienced lacked; and the Methodists covering a wide territory could raise many voices, loud ones too, against Catholic practices. The meager equipment necessary for a Methodist service allowed the Methodist preacher to scoff at the paraphernalia which was used at the Catholic Mass. It was the observation of a Tennessee historian that Methodists in that state were quick to cultivate a strong intolerance of Catholics. To them, so he said, "the cross was the emblem of Popish blasphemy, of the iniquity which masked as religion, as that religion that forbade the reading of the book of life, and encouraged the idolatrous worship of graven images." It became the traditional policy of the Methodist preachers to attack the Catholic Church, but they rarely made excursions into the realm of doctrines.

One single act may best reflect the growing animosity to Catholicism among the Methodists. An attempt was made at the General Conference in 1836 to delete the term "holy catholic Church" from the Apostles' Creed. The resolutions had been brought to the floor by Samuel Norris, a delegate from the New Hampshire Conference. After the motion was lost, Norris introduced a motion to append to the *Discipline* an explanatory note of the word "catholic." In response the conference saw fit to issue a definition of the term, spelling it out so simply that much of the odium was removed.

The Methodists continued to be uneasy in the presence of those Catholics who were deeply engaged in education of the youth. The General Conference of 1840 approved the publication in the West of a periodical designed for female readers. Its purpose was to counteract the influence of the Catholic literature and schools, for "as the foster parents of female minds and sentiment, [they] spare no pains in endeavoring to sway popular opinion. . . ."

In 1844 four bishops at the General Conference in a letter addressed to the British Conference, gave assurance that minds "imbued with evangelical principles" would withhold "the encroachments of Popery and semi-Popery," and would provide "an incongenial soil for the dogmas of Rome or Oxford." The Oxford Movement in the Episcopal Church had been bracketed with the Catholic threat; and, had not the slavery issue rent the Methodist Episcopal Church, the sentiments of the Oxford group would have continued to disturb Methodism in America. The division of the Methodist Church into Southern and Northern groups with subsequent formation in 1845 of the Methodist Episcopal Church, South, consumed for many years much of the energy of all Methodists.

The Oxford Movement which had begun in the Anglican Church in 1833 made little headway in America until the 1840's. The movement adopting the name "Anglo-Catholic" ushered in a period of bitter controversy in England and caused alarm in the Protestant Episcopal Church because of its likeness to Catholicism. In 1836 an Episcopal rector at Natchez, Mississippi, shifted to the Catholic faith; and a few years later the editor of a Vicksburg paper, recalling the instance of defection, described the steps that were leading the Episcopal Church "on her way to Rome." A much more significant case involved Levi S. Ives, Bishop of North Carolina, who in 1852 announced his "submission to the Catholic Church." Southern bishops immediately gave voice to their fears of the Oxford trend and admonished against any tendencies in that direction. Bishop Otey of Tennessee expressed "suspicion and alarm upon any act or object . . . that might symbolize the heresies of Rome." Bishop Cobbs of Alabama averred that the secession of Ives was probably a divine penalty for deviating too far "from the Protestant principle of the church . . . too much tampering with Romish books, doctrines and usages." He warned all clergymen "to abstain from the introduction of all novelties." Bishop Stephen Elliott of Georgia said, "Any man is in danger who becomes discontented with the Scriptural principles on which our Reformation was planted. . . ." Bishop William N. Green of Mississippi spoke out the most severely of all: "[Ives] has betrayed the most solemn trust ever committed to man, by renouncing his apostolic commission and throwing himself into the arms of Antichrist. . . ."

One church historian, in pointing out the unfortunate results that came from some innovations made by the High Church group, said: "It placed the Episcopal Church in a false attitude toward its contemporaries. It produced a timid, ecclesiastical temper." The worst effect, so he thought, lay in the loss of the "hospitable attitude" which the Episcopal Church had enjoyed with other denominations. The church was now "sadly distracted with the strife of tongues." The striking absence of Catholic comment on the movement gives evidence of its complete satisfaction with the direction which, for the time being, the Oxford group had taken.

Although the Baptist churches had no central organization to take a united action against the Catholics, the preachers expressed themselves in many and telling ways. The observations of two Baptist preachers appeared frequently in print and may well be taken as the opinion of a moderate and of an extremist. John M. Peck, widely known throughout the Mississippi Valley as editor of the *Western Pioneer and Baptist,* was generally regarded by all Protestants as a fair and generous critic of the times. In 1819 on a visit to New Orleans he wrote of the depressing state of religion, and, speaking of the Catholics, said: "The Catholick religion is the same in its spirit and tendency as in the fifteenth Century . . . ; it is still a *beast,* though in the United States without *horns."* Some twenty years later, Peck made a similar comment about New Orleans: "Here Catholic influence is felt in all its soporific influence, and nothing is comparatively done or attempted by Protestants to redeem this beautiful country. . . ."

One of the sharp thorns endured by the Catholics in Kentucky was William C. Buck, editor of the *Baptist Banner,* who delighted his readers by using such epithets as "Pope-ridden priest" and "advocate of Sabbath-breaking and Bible-burning" to describe the editor of the *Catholic Advocate.* To the aid of the Catholic editor rushed one who, calling himself "a Native Kentuckian," said the Baptist should not be censured too heavily, for "ignorance had a claim to sympathy." Insist not, he urged facetiously, upon grammar, rhetoric, or logic, but "admire bold and creative genius" in one who had preached for so many years in the Western forests. And indeed Buck's creative genius was at work, for he wrote articles depicting Popery as "a politico-religious despotism, antagonistic, alike, to all godliness and to all civil and religious freedom." Getting further agitated over the flood of immigrants, Buck denounced all of them as "sworn vassals of a foreign despot" aiming to get "most of the public interests in their hands." He continued in this vein, and at a later date wrote a column on "Papal Espionage" to which he attributed a scheme so well devised that every papist was bound to disclose everything he sees or hears that is "adverse to popery." Concerning the last tirade the Catholic editor commented succinctly, "Poor Brother Buck! he is in imminent danger of an attack of popomania."

All of the Protestant denominations feared the influence of the Catholic schools. Perhaps the Presbyterians felt the least resentment, for they had early assumed the role of educators; and the burden was heavy enough to share—even with the Catholics. Complaints were made that the capacity of the Catholic schools far exceeded the needs of the Catholics, and the grounds for such were justifiable because from one-half to two-thirds of all the pupils in their schools were Protestants. The Baptists viewed the whole system as a design to make proselytes and warned parents about ill-placed confidence. A correspondent to the *Baptist Banner* (February 16, 1843) asked, "How can we conscientiously send our children to Catholic schools to become Catholics or infidels, the almost invariable result of a residence at a Roman Catholic school, College, or Nunnery?" Although he gave his cause for alarm an irrational turn, the writer may well have been concerned over the impact which these schools were making upon the harsh anti-Catholic bias and prejudice. Satisfied patrons and nurtured children held the teachers and the schools in warm regard and expressed many debts of gratitude.

Much of the anti-Catholic sentiment came out of the East and was echoed in the West without genuine basis. In line with the usual observations of a "home-made" preacher, a Missouri correspondent to the *Western Recorder* (June 1, 1853) made some keen comments about young ministers with diplomas from Eastern seminaries who had been sent by a society to work in the same region with him. There was little reason, the writer insisted, to cherish the notion that the West would fall into the possession of the Catholics, for the menace did not exist. Step by step he outlined the wasteful program: young preachers having gotten the call to the West were dissatisfied with the meager equipment which awaited them, so they requested additional funds from their sponsoring organization. They had seen a few Catholic Irishmen and a few Catholic Germans, and effectively the young preachers made the horrors of Popery the theme of their appeal, recounting all the bloody annals of the past and describing the awful consequences to the West if Catholicism prevailed. People in the East were moved, and aid was given. The story was told over and over and grew with each telling.

The American Home Missionary Society of interdenominational origins had been organized in 1826 with the purpose of reaching the great unchurched masses who were in the West. By 1850 about one thousand missionaries were being sponsored in varying degrees throughout the Western region; but only a small number had been assigned to the South and the Southwest, for there the missionary smelled of Yankee sentiment and hinted of ulterior motives. The sentiment of Southern churches could have been no better expressed than in a query made in 1844 in the Alabama Baptist State Convention. The question asked: "Is is proper for us in the South to send any more money to our brethren at the North for missionary and other benevolent purposes before the subject of slavery be rightly understood by both parties?" This was one of several instances of discord that had led to the formation of the Southern Baptist Convention in 1845. Having achieved in some satisfactory measures its original purpose, the American Home Missionary Society with a fine working machinery had to seek fresh fields in order to justify its continuance. After viewing the influx of foreigners, many of whom were Catholics, the society turned its focus toward the Catholic Church, envisaged a growing menace, and directed its money and men toward holding the West for the Protestants. A careful sampling of hundreds of letters from the missionaries to officers of the society fails to reveal any significant danger arising from Catholics. About as many letters objected to the Disciples of Christ and the Mormons as to the Catholics. According to the opinion of a thorough student of this enormous correspondence, the so-called Catholic threat to Protestantism was "a fear based more on

Lincoln Christian College

the fancies of the Eastern religious leaders than on the actual experiences of the majority of the missionaries in the West."

Of all the preachers of the persuasion of the Disciples of Christ, only Alexander Campbell seems to have made any noticeable and effective attack on Catholicism. Having both the wit and the wisdom of a good controversalist, Campbell said pointedly what others would liked to have spoken. As a young man in Ireland, Campbell had known Catholics; and by hearsay and observation he had early formed the opinion that as a group they were an "ignorant, priest-ridden, superstitious people." On his first trip across the Alleghenies to his new home in America, he noted the absence of bolts and bars on the doors of an inn and irrationally attributed this security to the absence of many Catholics in Pennsylvania. Campbell, however, rarely jumped to such erroneous conclusions; so it might be safe to say he was intoxicated with the American scene.

Despite a noticeable rising opposition to the Catholic Church in the 1820's Campbell had little to say, for his reforms within the Presbyterian and Baptist churches required his undivided attention for several years. Later, after the new sect had taken definite form as the Disciples of Christ, Campbell initiated in 1833 his attacks on the Catholics by writing a series of eight articles on the "Catholic Controversy." By now he had been infected with the spirit of nativism and in this series dwelt on the danger to Americanism and Protestantism from the great influx of

Catholic immigrants. He was fearful of the schools supported by funds sent from Europe; and, as he magnified the threat to public education, he likewise magnified the sums of money. Taking encouragement from the reception of the articles, Campbell added some lectures on certain aspects of Catholicism to his repertory. He was a popular speaker and in great demand. Peculiarly enough Campbell did not shred Catholic personalities in the same ruthless manner he had attacked some of his Protestant rivals. The latter were more deserving of his opposition, so he said.

Significant recognition came to Campbell when some citizens of Cincinnati petitioned him to meet Bishop Purcell in debate on a religious subject. The idea was agreeable to both participants, and early in 1837 they engaged in a week-long discussion. By mutual arrangement the debates were to be stenographically recorded, printed in book form, and the proceeds from the sale to be divided equally between two designated charities. Since both men had a touch of the blarney, each defended his position ably and aroused excitement but no resentment, so that a long friendship followed this encounter.

Lesser lights than Campbell and Purcell were not able to maintain the high level of argumentation which the leaders had upheld. Excerpts from two church periodicals will show the sharp criticisms that were made in a wide time span. In 1837 the *Catholic Telegraph* (June 22) scathingly commented on Campbell's assumption of authority, and taking literary flight the writer apostrophized: "O

Luther, Calvin, Fox, Cranmer, Wesley, peace to your disappointed shades!" He declared that Christian Protestants should be glad to surrender to "the great Western Saint, Apostle, Prophet," and to discard all sects in favor of his regenerated primitive church. When the Campbell-Rice debates on baptism were published in 1844, the *Catholic Telegraph* (April 13, 1844) described the large volume, containing discussions which had consumed sixteen days: "A greater mass of invective, ignorance and folly was never yet heaped up; the appropriate commentary of a religion which makes the Bible the sole rule of faith, as each one understands it." It was the opinion of the writer that Campbell was so filled with "blind eyed ignorance" that he could not possibly injure the Presbyterians on whom he spat his venom. A Disciple correspondent to the *Christian Evangelist* (August, 1854) recounted his visit to the Cathedral in Louisville and described the repulsion which he felt as he examined the confessional. He had been "forcibly struck with the adaptiveness of all its contrivances to damnable deeds." Drawing fresh breath, he declared the confessional booth to be of such design that "the arch-enemy of God and man, in all the plenitude of his ingenuity, could not devise a more adroit mode of his work than by this infernal Institution."

In the face of such varied assaults made on them by the Protestant groups, the Catholics maintained excellent public relations. Of course, there were certain small areas that were exceptions; but these served to accentuate the prudence which characterized the behavior of the Catholics. They realized that they represented a very unpopular minority; and, while they willingly met a challenge, they did not attack the teachings of another religious group without provocation. The example set by Father Badin, Bishop Flaget, and Bishop Martin J. Spalding in early Protestant-Catholic relations in Kentucky became the standard for those who followed in their steps. In 1801 Father Badin had written to Bishop Carroll about the Baptist activities around him: "The Baptists continue to make much noise here. . . ." Then reporting to his superior, he added, "I preach peace, tho' they are very troublesome among Catholics. . . ."

The wide divergence between the education and training of a Roman Catholic priest and that of a Methodist preacher accounts in a large measure for the incompatibility that distinguished all their relations. The Catholics believed the Methodists were the noisiest of all preachers "particularly when they determine to create a revival." They looked upon the camp meetings as "heathenish assemblies" whose "demoralizing effect" has been proved. "What is the area around the camp," a Catholic writer asked, "but a scene for the exhibition of vice, where the profane swearer, the reeling drunkard, the rowdy, the pickpocket and such like to mix among the thousands who seek only amusement?" They wanted no part of the "Methodist holiday," which alternately amused and disgusted the Catholic observer.

It was a practice of the *Catholic Telegraph* and the *Catholic Advocate* to reprint articles that had appeared in some Protestant religious magazine. Frequently excerpts were presented in box, focusing attention without comment. The activities of the camp meetings were so spotlighted. A few specific examples will indicate the type of material selected. The *Telegraph* (March 6, 1845) quoted from the *Millennial Harbinger* a description of the participants in a camp meeting as they sat "looking vacantly into space, with that strange, wild, and indescribable sort of grining [*sic*] smile that we have seen upon the unfortunate inmates of those asylums benevolently provided for the insane." Catholic readers of the *Telegraph* (December 17, 1846) must have enjoyed a reprint from the *Western Christian Advocate* which recommended that a deputation of Methodist preachers should be sent to Rome, for a "camp meeting in the Coliseum would recall vividly to the minds of the astonished Italians, the Pagan times when the amphitheatre re-echoed to the roar of the lions." The *Catholic Advocate* (April 29, 1848) endorsed the sentiment which had been expressed in the *Western Baptist Review* concerning the effervescent effects of the revivals: "So soon as the extra action ceases, the flame dies away, the new leaven is corrupted by the old, and all immediately relapses into the former listless inactivity and coldness." The *Telegraph* (September 24, 1846) reprinted from the *Nashville Christian Advocate* a report of a revival, made remarkable by "a baptismal shower of fire."

The preacher singled out the convert he had made of a woman of the Disciples of Christ faith who chose to become "a passenger on the Southern Methodistical steamship, familiarly known as the 'Old Ship of Zion.' "

The formation in 1845 of a league of Protestant ministers in Louisville indicates that this organization was similar to the American Protestant Association which had been formed in Philadelphia in 1842. That pilot group was pledged "to awaken the attention of the community to the dangers which threaten the liberties . . . of these United States from the assaults of Romanism," and ministers everywhere were invited to join the crusade. The Louisville league was composed of three Presbyterians, two Baptists, and two Methodists who agreed to exchange pulpits for a "combined polemical attack" on the Catholics. Their joint efforts also produced *True Catholic,* a semi-monthly paper, which was designed for the same purpose. Later the headquarters of the magazine moved to Cincinnati, but the editorial policy remained the same. Large crowds attended the lectures, and the publicity which the Catholic Church received seemed to have had no damaging effect. The Presbyterians were not satisfied with their allies who they feared had hurt the cause of Protestantism. The bold light of inspection had not revealed the secrets which the Protestants had said were in Catholic doctrine and practice. There were some people in Louisville who thought the league had actually broken down prejudice against the Catholics. And the Catholics said that attendance at their churches had been sufficiently increased so that galleries were soon needed to accommodate the growing membership.

Resentment to the increasing number of foreigners coming to the United States in the 1840's encouraged the rising nativistic movement which entered American politics in the form of the American Republican Party, organized in New York in 1843. Two years later at a convention in Philadelphia, the party became the Native American Party, whose members, desiring a secret patriotic society, called themselves Know-Nothings. The new party desired to curtail immigration, to elect only native Americans to office, and to require aliens to reside in the United States for twenty-five years before becoming eligible for citizenship. Although the party officially opposed only those Roman Catholics who paid temporal allegiance to the Pope, many people attributed the formation of the Native American Party to a hatred of Catholicism. In the South the party was more antiforeign than anti-Catholic; this fact explains why native-born Catholics joined the party, particularly in Louisiana. Nevertheless, thousands of Protestants chose to accept the purported anti-Catholic origin of the Know-Nothings and often supported politicians who promised to destroy the menace.

After a few years considerable opposition to Know-Nothingism arose among some Protestants. Augustus B. Longstreet, a prominent Methodist preacher, judge, and editor in Mississippi, made it clear in 1855 when he addressed a group of Methodist preachers that, even if all the foreigners who came to the United States were Catholics and all voted under the dictation of the Pope, Know-Nothingism still would not be the proper remedy for the Protestants to apply. He pointed out the advantages of immigration and pleaded with the preachers to drop the movement and by doing so to bind all the South, all foreigners, all Catholics, and all Democrats against nativism. The Louisville *Democrat* (May 10, 1856) deplored a situation that would lead a Protestant minister "under cover of night, into some hiding place, and there surrounded by crafty politicians, infidels, blacklegs, and vagabonds of all sorts, exchange mutual pledges against the Pope and his religion."

It is not the purpose of this study to relate the involved connection of the nativistic movement to the Catholic-Protestant struggle in the South and the West. The Catholics suffered a great deal at the hands of a combination of antiforeign and anti-Catholic forces. A disturbance of religious services at Nashville, the bloody riot in Louisville, an attack on a medical school in St. Louis, the ransacking of a hospital in New Orleans, and assaults on convents in Galveston and Charleston attest to the intensity of this movement. Beyond question the effort of the nativists to enlist the support of Protestant denominations in the no Popery and anti-Catholic campaign won some affirmative response.

All in all, the foreign-born was not a serious problem

in the South; but many religious leaders generally regarded
his religion as a threat to Protestantism. By means of loud
voice and bold print, the menace of Catholicism became
increasingly clear, and the South's bitterness against the
foreigners mounted proportionately. In a few states the
degree of anti-Catholic bitterness, such as that in Tennessee, seemed to be illogical. There the acrid situation was
largely created by Parson Brownlow and his Knoxville
Whig, the most influential paper in East Tennessee. The
people in rural sections were especially susceptible to
propaganda and to rumors about foreigners, and Brownlow fed his readers on acetous fermentations. Since the
rural Southerners knew little or nothing about Romanism,
their natural reaction to the foreign implants was highly
unfavorable.

Through the 1840's and the 1850's Brownlow continued
in his newspaper to issue warnings against the Catholics
and to point out that they were voting the Democratic
ticket. While the Know-Nothing party was rising, he was
writing *Americanism Contrasted with Foreignism, Romanism, and Bogus Democracy*, which he published as a book
in 1856. Ruthlessly he characterized the Catholic Church
as a "dangerous and immoral corporation" which, "if
unchecked, will overturn the civil and religious liberties
of the United States." Through the use of simple arith-
metic, the Parson marshaled his facts against the Catholics
by saying that they had killed 68,000,000 people "for no
other offense than that of being Protestants." Assuming

that each slain person's body contained four gallons of blood, he reckoned that the bloody deluge would have been sufficient "to overflow the banks of the Mississippi, and destroy all the cotton and sugar plantations in Mississippi and Louisiana."

In contrast to Brownlow in Tennessee another "Parson" exhibited a very different attitude toward Catholics. Theodore Clapp, familiarly known in New Orleans as "Parson Clapp of the Strangers Church," went there in 1822 to assume the pastorate of a Congregational-Presbyterian church. Fresh from Yale College, Clapp said that he had come to his new work with "strong, blind, and hateful" prejudices against Catholics and had expected no pleasant relationship with them. As his opportunities for social contacts increased, he found the priests to be surprisingly "intellegent, enlarged, refined, and remarkably interesting in conversation." He cultivated their acquaintance, made intellectual excursions into their doctrine, and attended numerous High Masses. The cholera epidemic of 1832 provided the opportunity for him to witness the humanitarian conduct of the priests, all of whom stayed in New Orleans at a time when the city was being evacuated. Only two Protestant preachers had remained to serve the sick and the grieved—Clapp and a consumptive Episcopal rector who was too weak to leave his room. With death rampant, the priests had attended both Protestants and Catholics, altering their usual last rites to meet the specific need. Through warm personal experiences Clapp had witnessed the charity and devotion of the priests and the nuns; he had learned to appreciate the beauty of the service and the general efficiency of the religion.

For more than thirty years Clapp lived in New Orleans where about half of the Catholics in the South were concentrated. With his own eyes, he had seen at work the social forces which had effected "an accommodating Catholicism and a compromising Protestantism." When he traveled in New England, he was pained to hear Louisiana spoken of in terms of disparagement and was embarrassed by the remarks of a minister who could conceive of no worse calamity than having to spend his life in a state "encumbered by the corruptions of the Roman Catholic church." Clapp had seen people of all religious faiths live harmoniously in close proximity; it was not an impossible task if men would but try.

The small routines of everyday life called for little charity, little tolerance, and little understanding of unlikes. But when national disaster struck, men's bigotries paled into insignificance as they rallied to causes of large scope. As the Revolutionary War had brought Americans into new relationships, so the Civil War ushered in a brief cessation of sectarianism.

277.6
P85